THIS BOOK BELONGS TO

Loving God with All Your Mind

Elizabeth George

HARVEST HOUSE PUBLISHERS

EUGENE, OREGON

Cover by Dugan Design Group, Bloomington, Minnesota

Cover image © Antony Edwards/The Image Bank/Getty Images

Acknowledgment

As always, thank you to my dear husband, Jim George, M.Div., Th.M., for your able assistance, guidance, suggestions, and loving encouragement on this project.

LOVING GOD WITH ALL YOUR MIND
Copyright © 1994/2005 by Elizabeth George
Published by Harvest House Publishers
Eugene, Oregon 97402
www.harvesthousepublishers.com

Library of Congress Cataloging-in-Publication Data

George, Elizabeth, 1944–
  Loving God with all your mind / Elizabeth George.
     p. cm.
  Includes bibliographical references.
  ISBN 978-0-7369-1382-9 (pbk.)
  1. Christian women——Religious life. 2. God——Worship and love. I. Title.
  BV4527.G46 2005
  248.8'43——dc22   2004018775

Printed in the United States of America

09   10   11   12   13   14   / BP--CF /   16   15   14   13   12   11

To, for, and because of Jim

CONTENTS

INVITATION TO A CHANGED LIFE

❧

WOULD YOU LIKE *ALL* YOUR THOUGHTS to be pleasing to the Lord? Would you like to exchange doubt, discouragement, depression, and fear for energetic faith and joy? Would you like to know what to do and how to handle the next problem that comes your way? Then look to Jesus for the answer. In Matthew 22:37, He tells us to "love the Lord your God with all your heart, with all your soul, and *with all your mind.*" When you do this, you will indeed find your life changed—transformed! You will begin to...

- work on what is real...rather than worry about what is unreal.

- reach forward and press on...rather than remain a prisoner of the past.

- act on what is revealed in Scripture...rather than trust in your emotions.

What I offer in this book are six powerful Scriptures that have brought stability, strength...and sweet peace...into my life and into the lives of others. These Scriptures are guaranteed to be life-changing for you, too—because they come straight from God's Word!

Have you read the original version of *Loving God with All Your Mind?* Are you wondering, "Why this new volume?" The answer in a word is "growth." It's been ten years since this book was first published. During that time, I have grown spiritually. I have grown in my personal application of these six truths through new and different phases and events in my life. I have grown as I've shared these Scriptures in my conferences. And now I want to share this new growth and deeper understanding with you!

Thanks to the graciousness of Harvest House Publishers, what you hold in your hands is an update of what I trust you will find to be a transforming, inspiring, and encouraging book about the power of thinking on God's truth. It is substantially revised and filled with added insights and illustrations. It's language is practical and to the point. And because I understand your busy lifestyle, the chapters are shorter and more manageable. It also includes success stories and victories shared by others.

I also invite you and your Bible-study group to use the companion volume, *Loving God with All Your Mind Growth and Study Guide.* The additional Scriptures and the focus on personal application will further increase your spiritual growth and ignite your desire to love the Lord wholeheartedly.

I give thanks to God for the ministry this book has had so far. And I am praying that *your* life will be truly transformed as you think on these truths about God and look at life's challenges from God's perspective—through His Word. Then He will indeed change your thoughts...and your life! And you will find yourself truly loving God with all your mind.

In His everlasting love,

Elizabeth George

Training Your Thoughts

❧❦❧

Finally, brethren,

whatever things are true,

whatever things are noble,

whatever things are just,

whatever things are pure,

whatever things are lovely,

whatever things are of good report,

if there is any virtue and

if there is anything praiseworthy—

meditate on these things.

PHILIPPIANS 4:8

THINKING ON THE TRUTH

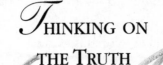

Whatsoever things are true...
think on these things.

PHILIPPIANS 4:8 KJV

*B*ECAUSE MY HUSBAND, JIM, IS IN the ministry, our phone rings a lot. And sure enough, one morning many years ago was no different. As I hurried across the family room to answer another call, I prayed my standard on-the-way-to-answer-the-phone prayer—"God, whoever it is, whatever it is, help me."

That prayer, however, did not prepare me for the startling request this caller made. The woman, a member of our church, explained that she had met with one of the pastors that morning because of her tendency toward depression. At the end of the counseling session, he had given her a homework assignment: "Go home and call Elizabeth George and ask her how she overcame her struggle with depression."

Overcoming Depression

Too shocked to respond, all I could do was ask for the woman's phone number and for some time to think about my answer. As I hung up the phone, a tidal wave of emotions swept over me.

First, I felt concern for this woman. So few Christians face their problems to the point of seeking advice. Even fewer actually show up for a prearranged appointment. Still fewer do what the counselor recommends. And here was a woman who had done it all! And she was asking me for help.

Next came distress. I didn't like hearing that someone was using my name in a counseling session. And I wasn't exactly thrilled to be characterized as someone who battled with depression, even though it was true. Besides, I thought I'd kept up a strong front...but obviously this pastor had seen through my facade. And, praise God, he had noticed some victory and headway!

Then came pain. As you read this book, you'll discover that one key to loving God with all your mind is choosing *not* to dwell on the past or on unpleasant memories. Yet to help this woman, I would need to once again look closely at the painful past. As I made myself remember those darker days, I recalled my morning routine....

Dark days—Every day I woke up in what I selfishly considered less-than-desirable surroundings—a tiny house in the middle of a desert with no air conditioning and no dishwasher. That meant that several times a day I had to stand in sweltering heat at the kitchen sink doing our dishes by hand. (That's enough to depress any woman!)

And there I stood, looking out the window and thinking long and hard while I washed dishes. Amazingly, I could recall almost every negative thing that had ever happened to me in my life! I thought about other days and better times. I relived unkindnesses and mistreatments. I reviewed again and again my failures and disappointments along with my dreams that, by the looks of things, were never going to come true. Soon my thoughts pulled me down so far that tears streamed down my cheeks and into the dishwater.

After the dishes came the housework. As I went from room to room, I felt oppressed and numb. A heavy, dark fog settled in my head. As I made each bed, I wanted to get into it, sink my head into the pillow, pull the covers up over my head, and close my eyes. You see, with my eyes shut, maybe—just maybe!—the fog would go away. Everything would be black, and I wouldn't have to keep groping my way along....

Remarkable change—"Exactly how had my life changed since those days?" I wondered and prayed. What had helped me get past those dark and heavy moods? What had freed me from that almost-immobilizing depression? Was there some key I could pass on, some hope and help I could offer? This dear lady needed to know.

I've learned in the past 20 years that I'm not alone. Others—like you perhaps?—also need help. I now know that...

- Some form of depression affects more than 17.5 million Americans each year.

- Depression can affect anyone, regardless of background, though major depression strikes women twice as often as men.

- More than 1 in 5 Americans can expect to get some form of depression in their life-time.[1]

Turning to God's Word

As I mentally journeyed back to those "dark days," I saw how God had worked in my life through three specific practices.

Memorizing God's Word—The first was hiding Scripture in my heart. As a new Christian, I was advised that I should memorize Scripture. And not knowing that I had an option, I dutifully began to memorize passages from God's Word. I wrote Bible verses on index cards and carried them with me in my purse, taped them on mirrors, and laid them on the breakfast table. And, especially important, I placed them on the windowsill over my kitchen sink. I was doing what I knew was right...but I was quite unaware of the great benefits I would reap.

Meditating on God's Word—The second habit I was cultivating was meditating on Scripture. I had learned some methods for reflecting on God's Word in several wonderful books.[2] Furthermore, the Scripture memory course I had enrolled in required meditation exercises for the assigned verses.[3] Again, I knew that I was doing what was right...but I didn't know how helpful meditating on Scripture would actually prove to be.

Applying God's Word—The third...and most challenging!...practice I was trying to master was obedience—
actually doing what God's Word said. I admit, it wasn't
always easy to do what God was telling me to do in the
verses I was memorizing and meditating on. But I knew
that God gave us His Word to show us how to live. And I
knew that I needed to *do* what it says, not just *know* what
it says (Matthew 7:21).

There was no way in the world to fathom at that time
the many ways God would use these three practices to
remove the bars of negative thinking that held me prisoner!

Thinking on "These Things"

One morning, as I was standing at my kitchen sink
washing dishes (again!), I was looking at the index card
that was propped up on the windowsill. The memory verse
laboriously written on it was Philippians 4:8. That's a
l-o-n-g verse about the eight virtues prescribed by God for
a Christian's thought-life. And it had been v-e-r-y hard for
me to learn. Anyway, as I reviewed the verse, I counted the
eight virtues on my fingers to make sure I didn't leave one
out:

> Finally, brethren, whatsoever things are true,
> whatsoever things are honest, whatsoever things
> are just, whatsoever things are pure, whatsoever
> things are lovely, whatsoever things are of good
> report; if there be any virtue, and if there be any
> praise, think on these things (KJV).

I had already spent time meditating on Philippians 4:8
as a whole, so I knew it was a guideline for the kinds of

thoughts God desired to occupy my mind. But I had never thought about each component separately. And that morning I decided to take the verse apart while I washed the dishes. Going through an exercise designed for discovering the meaning of Scripture, I said out loud, "Finally, brethren, whatsoever things are true." Then I stopped and asked, "What does *true* mean?" And my answer? "Obviously *true* means truth, the truth of Scripture. And *true* means the truth as opposed to lies. But *true* also means real, because what is true is what is real."

The door of understanding cracked open for me!

Continuing on with the exercise, I asked, "Is there a command to obey?" I recited my way through the entire verse again and landed on God's command at the end of it —*think on these things*. Stated in the positive, God is issuing the command to "let your mind dwell on what is true or real." And stated in the negative, the same command would be "Do not think on things that are not true or real."

Suddenly God's Word seemed to be screaming at me, "Elizabeth, *stop* thinking on things that are not true and real!"

Breaking Through

And there it was! "Whatsoever things are true...think on these things." In just eight words—*eight* words!—out of the fathomless treasure of God's Word, I had my breakthrough. It came when I realized that God did not want me to spend my precious time and equally precious mental energy thinking on things that are not true or real.

As I sought to apply this instruction and obey the command of Philippians 4:8, the darkness over my life began

to lift and the light of God's Word flooded into my heart,
soul...and mind! Here, in a mere handful of words, God
was telling me not to think about anything that wasn't true
or real, and I needed to be faithful in putting this truth into
practice.

Here's something for us to think about. It's been esti-
mated that 10,000 thoughts pass through the human mind
in one day. Obeying God's command to filter our thoughts
through His grid of *true* and *real* is no easy task. But,
thanks be to God, He helps us accomplish whatever He
asks us to do!

Making Progress

Encouraged—and excited!—about my discovery, I
started to evaluate my daily thoughts in light of the first few
words of Philippians 4:8. I literally had to train my
thoughts. I had to make it a point to ask myself, "Am I
thinking on the truth—on what is true and real?"

Over the next few weeks, as I continued to ask this
question, I made some dramatic progress in changing my
thought-life. I also began to realize that God had a solution
for my long struggle with depression and worry and fear.
For the first time, I understood that His Word offered hope
for my moodiness! That solution, and that hope, lay in
keeping my thoughts within the biblical boundaries of
Philippians 4:8—"Whatsoever things are *true* [or *real*]...
think on these things."

These few words helped me take a significant first step
toward spiritual mental health. And this scripture continues,
to this day, to correct all my unhealthy thinking. And it can
do the same for you.

Realizing Strength for Daily Life

Take it from me, blessings abound when you and I think on what is true and real. And one of those blessings is strength for daily life—strength that includes energy, health, and vitality. Let me explain. I'm sure you know how limited you are when you are ill. Well, when you aren't functioning according to what is real, it's like trying to do something when you have a fever or the flu. Even though you force yourself to fulfill your responsibilities, something is missing. Your body's ability and the demands of each task are out of sync! Sure, you go ahead and do your work, but there is little, if any, enthusiasm. And many times your work is half done or done poorly. Why? Because of poor physical health...which means less energy...and even less performance.

The same thing happens in the spiritual realm! Like a virus, your thoughts can drain your energy and cripple your usefulness. But, praise God, the opposite is also true. Your thoughts can be a source of strength. When you think on the powerful truths of Scripture, God uses His Word to change your way of thinking. And one beneficial—and much-needed!—result is that you are strengthened and energized for daily life by thinking on the truth—on what is true and real.

Loving God...Even More _____

As I think about you as the reader of a book bearing the title *Loving God with All Your Mind,* I am assuming that you already love God. As a believer in Christ, you have already responded to God's love for you. As a truth in the Bible

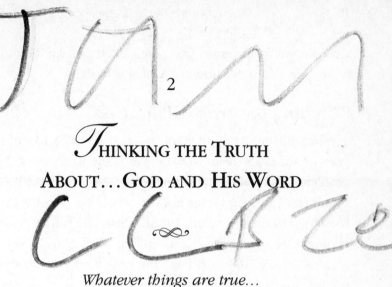

2

$\mathcal{T}$HINKING THE TRUTH ABOUT…GOD AND HIS WORD

Whatever things are true…
meditate on these things.

PHILIPPIANS 4:8

$\mathcal{D}$EAR READER, I PRAY THAT a transformation has already begun in your heart and mind…as it did in this woman's life:

> Elizabeth, what ministered to me most from your teaching on "Loving God with All Your Mind" is thinking on what is true and real. As a sufferer of depression, I now think on what is true and real, and trust God and His Word rather than spiraling down into despair and suicidal depression. This is totally new to me!

I'm also praying that you are grasping the importance of training your thoughts to think on what is true and real. For me it was the first step in learning what it means to love

God with all your mind. And here's another step: We must be thinking thoughts about *God* that are true.

Thinking the Truth About God

Through my years of ministry, one scenario has often been repeated. A dear woman will come to me with her problem. Then, after she's poured out her heart, she'll say something like, "God must not care about me. He must not see how I'm being treated. He must not know what's happening to me. If He did, He would do something about it!" And then I can almost predict the next words: "God must not love me."

I never condemn or judge anyone who says these things. That's because I've felt this way, too. And I've said all of those things myself! But I've also learned that whenever you and I feel this way...or begin to think in this way...we must stop and ask, "But what is true and real about *God?*" We can then recall truths from the Bible that confirm God's love for us, His people. Truths such as these...

God cared for the Israelites—One year I set a goal to read through my Bible...and I made it all the way to Exodus, chapter 2! It was there that I witnessed and marked heavily in my Bible how God demonstrated His care for the Israelites. Here's what happened in Exodus 2. After Joseph died, the children of Israel were mistreated by the new pharaoh. Under severe persecution, they felt (as perhaps you have) that God didn't care about them. The Bible, however, reports that this was never the case. Even while the Israelites thought they were unloved and forgotten,

God *heard* their groaning, and God *remembered* His covenant....And God *looked* upon the children of Israel, and God *acknowledged* them (Exodus 2:24-25).

God indeed saw His people, and He took notice of their condition! And, far from forgetting them, God was well aware of His covenant with them. Then God acted on what He heard, saw, and noticed. He told Moses, "I have surely *seen* the oppression of My people...and have *heard* their cry...for I *know* their sorrows....So I have come down to *deliver* them...and I will send you" (3:7-10).

This God-breathed, true account from the Bible reminds us that God sees, hears, and knows all about the sufferings of His people. He also remembers His promises, cares about His people, and acts on their behalf and for their good. You and I must choose to "think on these things"—these comforting, tender, and rock-solid, never-changing truths about God's care and concern for us—rather than focus on our own faulty thoughts or feelings. Regardless of the difficulty and pain of life's circumstances, "these things" are what is true and real about God!

God cared for Hagar—The story of God's concern for Hagar is a favorite of mine. Twice God met this woman in times of great distress. At the first meeting, Hagar was pregnant, alone, and a fugitive. But "the Angel of the LORD found her" and said, "the LORD has *heard* your affliction" (Genesis 16:7,11). After her encounter with God, Hagar referred to Him as "You-Are-*the-God-Who-Sees*" (verse 13). Later, she had a son whom Abram named Ishmael, meaning *"God hears"* (verse 15).[1] Both Hagar and Abram recognized the truth that our God is truly a God who sees and hears...and cares! Hagar personally experienced His care, concern, and provision.

Hagar's second recorded meeting with God occurred 16 years later, and it, too, was initiated by Him. Although time had passed, God still knew, saw, heard, cared, and provided for this single mother. In this scene, Abraham had sent Hagar and her son away. In the blazing, bone-dry desert, the two of them were dying. Yet "God *heard* the voice of the lad" crying and provided the two of them with water as well as encouragement (Genesis 21:9-19).

God cares for you—When I think about the God who heard, saw, knew, and rescued the Israelites and Hagar, my faith in God's caring and concerned nature is strengthened. Then, when I add the truth of 1 Peter 5:7—"He cares for you"—the teaching is clear: God cares about and for His people. And that, dear reader, includes you and me!

Thinking the Truth About God's Word

Another crucial step toward loving God with all our mind is determining to place the Bible's truths above everything we think or feel. For instance, the Bible sets forth the important truth that "if we confess our sins, He is faithful and righteous to forgive us our sins and to cleanse us from all unrighteousness" (1 John 1:9 NASB). Although this statement guarantees that God forgives our sins, I've been guilty of saying, after a time of prayer and confession, "But I don't *feel* forgiven." When I do this, I am allowing my *feelings* to take precedence over the rock-solid, doctrinal truth of the forgiveness of sins available to us through Christ.

On other occasions I say, "But I don't *think* God could really forgive me." With a statement like this, I'm allowing my *thoughts* to take precedence over the Word of God.

My friend, you and I, as believers in Christ, are forgiven, regardless of our feelings and thoughts. That's that! In Christ "we have redemption through His blood, the forgiveness of sins" (Colossians 1:14). To think we are not forgiven is to think a lie, to think something that is untrue. Therefore, when my feelings and thoughts are running counter to what Scripture teaches, I need to stop and ask, "But, Elizabeth, what is true?" The answer is always the same: "The Bible is true, not my feelings or my thoughts." Therefore I choose to "think forgiven."

After I shared the truth of 1 John 1:9 at a Christian women's conference, one woman wrote, "For a long time now, my thoughts have been, 'But I don't feel forgiven' or 'Was I really saved to begin with?' I have confessed my sin over and over, and I hassle with it constantly. Reviewing the principle of thinking on the truth and this scripture is already beginning to correct my thinking."

Thinking the Truth About Ourselves

Another important guideline for our thoughts is we must think on the truth about ourselves. When we view ourselves through the lens of God's Word, we better understand God's love for us and the worth we have in His eyes. For example, Romans 5:8 tells us that "Christ died for us." This truth means that we are of inestimable value, precious in His sight...even when we don't feel or think we are. Such a truth teaches us about our position before God in Christ. Truths like these enable us to experience the power of God instead of suffering from the draining effects of thoughts about ourselves that simply are not true.

A personal story—I admit that I have to fight this battle against thinking negatively—and wrongfully!—about myself almost daily. But I well remember one day when the struggle was tougher than usual. I had accepted a writing assignment that challenged me to venture *way* beyond my comfort zone! However, confident of God's leading, I tackled the job. I worked harder and longer than ever...only to have my writing meet with strong reaction, resistance, and near rejection. I was mortified! I had failed!

Drained physically as well as emotionally, I crawled home to hide and recover. But even there, in the safety and shelter of my home-sweet-home, thoughts like these filled my mind: "Who do you think you are? When are you going to learn that you are nobody! You are nothing! When will you understand that the kind of ministry you were attempting is reserved for others who are better than you?"

As the day went on, my thoughts became even darker. "Why don't you just quit now? Why try? Why care? It was just a dream. And besides, you are a nobody and a nothing!"

I knew the signs all too well. I was sliding down into the dark hole of depression, defeat, discouragement, dismay, and dejection. But I began to fight back! I decided it might help if I got out of the house. So I went for a walk. But walking didn't help this time. With each step up our huge hill, I continued to hear the defeating chorus that had been there all day long.

But then the Holy Spirit broke through my relentless chant and prompted me to ask myself the key question: "But Elizabeth, what is true and real?" And, my friend, the answers from Scripture that God brought to my poor exhausted mind and heart came to my rescue! God reminded me that...

- I am fearfully and wonderfully made, no matter what I or others may think about me (Psalm 139:14),

- He has a grand plan and purpose for my life, no matter how the present may look (2 Timothy 1:9),

- He has given me spiritual gifts that I can use to benefit other believers, no matter how I may be floundering or failing at the moment (1 Corinthians 12:7-11), and

- I am always loved and accepted by God, no matter what I experience or who may reject me (Romans 8:35).

These thoughts are God's unshakable truth! And one by one, I began replacing my untrue thoughts with these *facts* —these *truths* from God's Word about how *He* sees me and about what *He* has accomplished on my behalf. And with each thought, each truth, God gave me His fresh strength and joy.

A personal friend—Another common error in our thinking is dwelling on unmet expectations. My friend Louise suffers from the crippling effects of rheumatoid arthritis and has to constantly guard her expectations for herself. Her unending pain and fatigue can cause her to dwell on what she can't do or on what she thinks she should be accomplishing. However, when this kind of thinking begins, Louise reports, "It comforts me to remember that God is all-knowing and has a plan for me that includes my condition. I find rest as I trust in Him because He is faithful and will do what He promises."

A personal word of encouragement—And for you, dear friend? Be assured that the same is true. When you think on God's Word, on what is true and real about yourself and your circumstances (as Louise does and as I'm learning to do), God uses His truth to break the cycle of destructive thinking that leads to discouragement, despair, doubt, and depression. However real the pain, the hurts, and the disappointments of your life are, you must remember the *greater* reality of God's love, power, and redemption. This brings God's comfort, healing, and hope to your heart and soul.

So...whenever you slip into thinking of yourself as useless, as worthless, as a failure, a hopeless case, or a loser, remember what is true:

- You are a child of God (John 1:12).

- You are His workmanship (Ephesians 2:10).

- You have been bought by the precious blood of Christ (1 Corinthians 6:20; 1 Peter 1:18-19).

Loving God...Even More

Throughout this chapter I've shared from God's Word, from my life, and from the lives of others. But now I'm wondering about you. What untrue thoughts about God do you find yourself entertaining? What truths and teachings in the Bible do you fail to accept and apply to your life as truth? And what debilitating thoughts do you tend to think about yourself...thoughts that don't match up to God's view of you as His child?

Oh, how I want you to understand the importance of training your mind to think on what is true and real! To love God with all your mind! When you do, what happens? You experience the joy and hope of being God's child. And blessings upon blessings, you experience spiritual encouragement, powerful enablement, and fresh energy for handling life as the Holy Spirit uses God's Word in your heart and mind!

That's what happened to the woman who wrote the letter at the beginning of this chapter. Read now how she concluded her triumphant, victorious note:

> I have been a slave to my roller-coaster emotions rather than keeping my eyes on God and trusting Him despite what my emotions are telling me. The Lord has given me so much strength and hope through His Word, despite how I feel. And you know what? When you keep your eyes on God and the Word of God, He gives you a peace

in your heart and hope which results in a quiet inner joy.

Dear heart, may the peace of God that surpasses all understanding keep and guard *your* heart and mind through Christ Jesus as you think on what is true and real.

3

$\mathscr{T}$HINKING THE TRUTH ABOUT...OTHERS

❧

Whatever is true...
think about such things.

PHILIPPIANS 4:8 NIV

$\mathscr{D}$O YOU SUFFER FROM AN OVERACTIVE MIND when it comes to thinking about your relationships? Most people do. And if that's the case for you, Philippians 4:8 can help. That's because your relationships with people also need to be guided by its truth: "Whatsoever things are true [or real]...think on these things" (KJV).

Playing Mind Games

I confess that through the years I've been guilty of playing mind games with people and second-guessing their motives. It's all too easy to wonder about what a person *isn't* saying or try to read between the lines of what he or she *does* say—"He says he loves me, but I don't think he does" or "She said there's nothing wrong, but I'm not so sure."

Isn't it amazing how we can come up with *very* creative explanations for people's actions? For example, "He's been grumpy lately, so he must be angry with me." We can also draw conclusions about why people do what they do— "She left a message on my machine to call her. I must have done something wrong" or "I wonder what she wants from me now." We can even apply this kind of thinking to what people do *not* do—"She hasn't called me in a while. I must have done something to offend her."

Well, there's help and hope for our imaginations *and* for our relationships! Two principles from Scripture can help settle such mind games.

Understanding the Principle of Love

The first principle is based on 1 Corinthians 13, on the apostle Paul's words about love. As he writes to his friends, Paul notes that love "thinks no evil" and "believes all things" (verses 5 and 7). One day I realized that I was violating these two requirements for love whenever I questioned what another person said or did. My habit of second-guessing involved interpreting—and even distorting—the words and actions of others. When I tried to read things into a person's words and actions rather than accepting them at face value, I was essentially making that person a liar.

The solution? I needed to stop my wild, speculative thoughts by asking myself, "But, Elizabeth, what is true and real?" The answer to this question then called me to believe what the other person said.

Putting the Principle of Love to Work

Learning to think no evil about another person and believe what he or she says has helped me make giant strides in my interaction with others. It has helped me eliminate second-guessing and reading between the lines. It has also diminished the misunderstanding and hurt that can come as a result of such untrue thinking. If he says he loves me, I now believe that he loves me. If she says it doesn't matter, I believe that it doesn't matter. If he says nothing is wrong, I believe that nothing is wrong. I think on what is true.

Let me quickly say that this is not always as easy as it sounds! One evening, after a class on this very principle from 1 Corinthians 13, a college student admitted her struggle. She shared, "Even though my friend seems to be avoiding me and not talking to me as much as before, I'm trying not to assume anything. Instead, I'm praying about it and, as 1 Corinthians 13:7 says, believing the best. It's hard, though, because my mind almost automatically wants to assume the worst."

A friend of mine told me about a similar situation. "When spending time with friends, I found myself being too sensitive and taking things they did and said out of context. But I am learning to take things at face value and to distinguish between what is perceived and what is real."

Like both of these growing Christians, you can break the habit of destructive thought patterns that damage relationships. Simply ask yourself, "What is true?" This exercise can help you stop the second-guessing, the analysis, and the introspection that hinder the development of healthy relationships.

Understanding the Principle
of a Clear Conscience

In Matthew 18:15, Jesus offers another principle for healthy relationships. He says, "If your brother sins against you, go and tell him his fault between you and him alone." The primary application of this truth is to simply obey the command and go to any person who sins against us.

But think for a minute about what this command means for you and me when other believers obey it. It means that when we sin against others, they are to come to us in private to talk about it.

I can't begin to describe the freedom this truth has given me! Because of it, I've quit wasting time and energy worrying about what other people think of me or about what I do. I've also stopped wondering what others *might* be thinking...or what I *might* have done wrong. Why? Because if I've done something wrong, they are to come to me and tell me. Until that happens, my guesses are just that. They're guesses...rather than fact, reality, or truth.

As I've stopped analyzing my every move and second-guessing other people's ideas about me, I have experienced more peace and greater openness in my relationships. I no longer fear or dread encounters with people. I've stopped wondering what critical thoughts they might be thinking. And I've begun

...looking to God through prayer,
...looking to His Word, and
...looking to mature Christian mentors

to reveal any wrong attitudes and actions rather than constantly looking for fault in things I've said or done.

Putting the Principle of a Clear Conscience to Work

Hear now the wisdom of Proverbs 28:1: "The wicked flee when no one pursues, but the righteous are bold as a lion." My paraphrase of this truth is, "If you haven't done anything wrong, don't act like it!" We are to boldly and confidently proceed in our relationships, rather than holding back, wondering what people are thinking about us. And this takes conscious effort, as one student discovered and wrote about in her class paper:

> A certain person was acting differently toward me. Normally I would have probed and speculated a lot, but I decided to act as if everything were okay. The next day she told me that she was dealing with some things and was sorry she had treated me badly. So [her behavior] wasn't because of something I had done after all.

Applying God's Principles to Your Thoughts

What kinds of thoughts do you tend to have about people? I doubt that they are always pure, positive, and prayerful. No one's are! After all, who hasn't slipped into second-guessing, analysis, and suspicion? And who hasn't been plagued by self-doubt or crippled by negative thoughts, insecurity, and worry? Instead of such unhealthy, cynical thinking, applying God's principles to your thoughts—

✓ Choose to think on what is true and real.

✓   Corral your thoughts and refuse to second-
     guess or draw conclusions about people's
     behavior.

✓   Count on others to tell you if you have
     failed in your behavior.

✓   Count on God's Spirit to point out when
     you have offended someone.

Do you want to nurture love and confidence in your
relationships with others? Then changing your thought-life
is key! By God's grace and with His help, choose to think
no evil about people. Determine to trust what others say
and do. Count on others to come to you when you have
failed them and count on God to reveal where you have
offended them. Thoughts about people that are based on
what is true and real will liberate you to generously and
joyously love and serve one another. That's what the Christian life is all about!

Tapping into the Power of God's Word

We've covered a lot of ground and addressed many of
our everyday problems. But before we step into a new
chapter about other issues and concerns that every human
must deal with, I want us to return to the basic truth of the
power of God's Word to help us in any and all of our life
experiences. So let's review...and remember these two
facts.

The foundation for a healthy thought-life is God's Word.
God has chosen to communicate with us through the Bible.
Therefore, His Word is to take priority over everything else
we might choose as the basis of our thoughts, actions, and
feelings.

The power God extends to us through His Word—and through thinking on His Word—can lift us out of the depths of defeat, discouragement, despair, doubt, dread, and depression and enable us to deal with the challenges that come our way.

With our thoughts based on the Word and Person of God, we find strength, hope, joy, faith, and peace of heart, soul, and mind. Then, as we encounter the events life brings our way, we will experience victory. Freed from the faulty mental habits that cripple our thought-life, we will be able to move calmly and steadily forward with courage and confidence.

An example of God's power to others—The story Ruth Graham tells about her parents illustrates the power that comes with thinking biblical truths, from thinking on God's Word. Dr. and Mrs. Nelson Bell ministered in China for 20 years during a time in China's history that was characterized by unrest and political and military upheaval. At one point, this faithful couple lay in their dugout shelter, not knowing their fate. The situation appeared to be hopeless, and these missionaries could easily have been overwhelmed by panic and despair. The choice was theirs...and they chose to view their situation through the lens of God's truth. Mrs. Bell reports:

> We were counting over our defenses....Overhead are the overshadowing wings (Psalm 91:4); underneath are the everlasting arms (Deuteronomy 33:27); all around "the angel of the Lord encampeth round about them that fear Him, and delivereth them" (Psalm 34:7); inside, that "peace which passeth all understanding" (Philippians

4:7); also, "Thou wilt keep him in perfect peace, whose mind is stayed on Thee: because He trusteth in Thee" (Isaiah 26:3).[1]

The Bells' focus on God's truth calmed their hearts and strengthened them to endure the challenges they faced.

Loving God...Even More

*M*y dear reading friend, the same assurances and power that sustained Dr. and Mrs. Bell are available to you! You can choose to think thoughts about God and life's situations that are *not* true...or you can choose to love God with all your mind and think the truths stated in Scripture. The next time you feel yourself slipping from confidence to cowardice, from control to emotion, from the strength of spiritual mental health to frailty of spirit, review the resources you have as a child of God. In times of trauma and testing, choose to fill your mind with what is true. Choose to love God.

And when it comes to your thoughts about others again put the power of God's Word to work! Instead of spending your time and mental energy analyzing other people's words and actions or second-guessing what they say and do, think on what is true and real. When you train your thoughts to focus in this way, you experience wonderful peace of mind and heart *and* sound and sincere connections and communications with others. As a result, your relationships become characterized by genuine love, a love for others that finds its source in your desire to love God...even more.

4

$\mathcal{T}$HINKING THE TRUTH
ABOUT...THE FUTURE

Whatever is true...dwell on these things.

PHILIPPIANS 4:8 NASB

$\mathcal{W}$HENEVER I TEACH OR SPEAK, I usually announce that I'm available afterward for any questions. One particular evening, a woman cautiously approached me after our class time. As she began talking, and well before she got to her question, I realized I was hearing someone share her deepest fears.

I had very little eye contact with this lady whose head hung so low. Her gripping fear constricted her breathing, which explained the labored whisper. When she did dare to look up, I saw intense pain in her eyes. Hers was a face robbed of the smile lines God meant her to have. Stress was taking its toll, and my heart ached for this woman in her anguish. God's desire is that she might live "abundantly"

(John 10:10), yet fear was robbing her of joy, as it does many of God's people.

Crippling Fear

As I've listened to others—and to my own heart and mind—I've realized that crippling fear comes to us for a variety of reasons. Here's a handful of fears...and I'm sure you can add to the list!

Disasters—In California, where I lived for 30 years, earthquakes cause everyone great concern. Newcomers to the state asked, "How do you know when you're having an earthquake? What does it feel like?"

"Oh, you'll know when it happens," I always said. And they did!

Finances—The prospect of not enough money or a loss of employment generates worry and fear. Add to these anxieties other crippling thoughts such as "I'm afraid we're going to lose our home" and "I'm afraid the economy will never improve," and it's easy to see how fear breeds more fear.

Child-raising—All parents experience fear for their children. First, we worry during pregnancy about a baby's development and safe delivery. After birth, a baby brings money worries and the loss of a more carefree lifestyle. As the baby grows, fears increase as parents worry about accidents, abuse, crime, school environments, pollution, war, and the future of the world. And top on our list is wondering whether our children will come to love Christ and follow Him so they will enjoy eternal life.

Then, when our children are adults, we worry about their choices of marriage partners, the new couple's finances, the possibility of divorce. And when the grand-children arrive, sure enough, the cycle of fear begins all over again.

Singleness—Many singles fear a lifetime of being alone. I'll never forget a young woman who attended a singles' Bible study in our home. When Amy mentioned that the next meeting would be on her birthday, the group instantly began planning a party for her at the end of our next study. The plans, however, were interrupted when Amy sobbed, "But you don't understand. This is not an occasion to cele-brate. I'm going to be 30!" To Amy, her birthday meant another year, another five years, another decade, had passed—and she was still single.

And here's another fact: Even those who are married often fear the singleness of divorce and widowhood.

Aging, illness, and suffering—During his ministry to senior citizens at our former church, Jim regularly heard dear saints express their fears of old age and of needing convalescent care in later years without adequate finances.

And many people—myself included—fear illness and suffering. But I found great hope when I watched my friend Allison, who suffers from multiple sclerosis (MS). Our seminary wives' fellowship group prayed with her through her medical tests and the diagnosis and witnessed Allison's initial struggles. Then, as she began adjusting to a new kind of life, we tried to help out. One evening we wept together as Allison shared a devotional based on James 1:2-4. In that passage, James writes:

> My brethren, count it all joy when you fall into various trials, knowing that the testing of your faith produces patience. But let patience have its perfect work, that you may be perfect and complete, lacking nothing.

Now hear Allison's message! Months before she and her husband came to the seminary, the women in her home church had studied James. Feeling stagnant as a Christian, Allison had read these first verses and prayed, "God, give me an opportunity to grow. Give me the opportunity to apply these truths in my life."

Next came the diagnosis of her disease.

As she faced MS, Allison changed her prayer to, "God, give me joy in my trial." She began a "Journal of Joy" and one entry read, "God, I can have joy and thank You because my illness was not a brain tumor." Seeing how Allison dealt with her illness reminded me that God is with us when we are sick or disease-ridden.

Death and dying—Closely related to the fear of illness is the fear of death. We wonder, "When will I die? How will I die? Will I suffer with dignity?" Too rarely do we have the apostle Paul's perspective on death in our minds. In his letter to the Philippians, Paul explains, "To die is *gain*" (Philippians 1:21). He teaches that to die is simply "to *depart* and *be with Christ*" (1:23) and that to be with Christ "is *far better*" (1:23). As an unknown poet has written, "Better, far better, with Christ to be, living and loved through eternity."

Overcoming Fear

What can we do to overcome our fears? How can we keep fear from robbing today of its joys? What can we do to control this raging and damaging emotion? And how can we stop thinking thoughts that hurt us and hinder our strength? Again, Scripture comes to our rescue. Considering the fact that fear is generally rooted in thoughts about things that are *not real,* we must again remember the admonition of Philippians 4:8—"Whatever things are true [or real]...meditate on these things."

As we've already noted, the first few words of Philippians 4:8 challenge us to think on what is true or real, to function according to facts, not feelings or fantasies. What we think must be...

- true according to what the Bible says,

- true according to the character of God as revealed in the Bible, and

- true according to what people say and do.

As we think on God's Word, He uses it to help us handle what is true and real and to calm our fears about the future, the past, and the present. Here's how.

Thinking About the Future

Do you frequently find yourself asking, "What if...?" That question can generate all kinds of fear about the future. Philippians 4:8, however, teaches that our thoughts should "belong to the nature of reality."[1] This guideline rules out all fearful dwelling on the future. God commands us to think on what is true and real. And it's a fact—events in the future are neither.

Our theme verse—Philippians 4:8—is a challenge to learn not to probe the future with fear-generating questions such as What if I never get married? What if I lose my spouse? What if I get cancer? What if my children rebel? Questions like these can consume our minds and keep us from loving and trusting God.

That was the case with Patty, a woman I met at a church retreat. As I spoke, I spotted Patty's distraught face in the audience. At one of the breaks, she came up to me and explained that she and her husband had wanted a baby for more than ten years. They were thrilled when God blessed them with a baby—but now it was time for the baby's DPT immunization. Having read about the mortality rate linked to DPT shots, this mother was postponing the shot. She voiced her fear to me: "What if my baby dies from that injection?"

Oh, dear friend, whatever your "what if" is, you must remember that "what if" is a guess. If you want to overcome your fears, you cannot think "what if" thoughts. Instead, in obedience to Philippians 4:8, you and I must acknowledge that events in the future are not real. We must eliminate this kind of speculative thinking because thoughts about the future are only guesses.

Furthermore, the future is in God's hands—His loving, capable, merciful, powerful hands! He can enable us to deal with what is real, with what is now. And, the truth is, He will also be with us whatever the future holds. Lo, He is "with you always, even to the end of the age" (Matthew 28:20)! Yes, we need to be prepared for things like earthquakes. And yes, we need to be wise about our finances, our parenting, and our health. But we don't need to waste energy worrying about what is not yet real, about things that may never come to pass.

Asking, "But What Is True and Real?"

We're extremely well-acquainted with fears-on-end, aren't we? But what does God say about these worries? Consider again, item by item, the list of fears we just looked at. Each one was a "what if" concern. Not one of the events was real. Not one of them had actually happened.

Disasters—Possible calamities (including earthquakes!) exist only in the mind...until they happen!

Finances—Potential money problems aren't today's money problems. Instead of worrying, we need to remember David's testimony in Psalm 37:25: "I have not seen the righteous forsaken, nor his descendants begging bread."

Child-raising—Similarly, a parent's worries about the future are not real. Instead of "forward worrying," we parents are to focus our energy on what we must do *today* because today is real. God asks parents to nurture, train, and discipline their children *today* (Ephesians 6:4)...and then wake up tomorrow and do the same. Being overly concerned about potential parenting problems saps our energy and our joy and interferes with our efforts as parents. God calls us to handle each day, one at a time. *Today* is real, and, beloved, God will enable us to deal with what today holds. That is what's true!

Singleness—This same principle holds for singles like Amy. God doesn't ask single adults to look down through the corridors of time future and imagine that they will be single forever. Again, He calls a single person to address what is real, and what is real is singleness *today*.

Although Amy's desire may be to be married, she—like you and I—can learn much from the wise words of missionary Jim Elliot. While waiting on God's will regarding marriage, Jim Elliot wrote to his future wife, Elisabeth Howard, "Let not our longing slay the appetite of our living." Commenting on this wisdom decades later, Mrs. Elisabeth Elliot wrote, "We accept and thank God for what is given, not allowing the *not-given* to spoil it."[2] God is adequate.

And what about worrying about singleness through widowhood? Even though widowhood is a possibility, God does not want a married person to ruin today's joy with his or her spouse by entertaining the thought of death. Why worry? God is, always has been, and always will be, sufficient.

Aging, illness, and suffering—God also offers His presence and provision to those who fear old age with the promise that "even to your old age...and even to gray hairs I will carry you!...I will carry, and will deliver you" (Isaiah 46:4). It's a fact...and a promise: God will take care of you and me in our later years.

Illness and suffering? God doesn't want our fear of possible physical suffering to overshadow the reality of our health and usefulness today. If and when we do experience physical trials, God will be with us through them, and we will find, with Paul, that we "can do all things through

Christ who strengthens me" (Philippians 4:13). God will strengthen us.

Death and dying—Death is the ultimate reality for everyone, but it is also the ultimate victory for every Christian. The Bible says "to be absent from the body" is "to be present with the Lord" (2 Corinthians 5:8). Fearing death and dying can keep us from living full and productive lives today. But we can surrender that fear to God's promise that He will be with us "through the valley of the shadow of death" (Psalm 23:4). God is and will be present with us.

Did you notice a pattern in these suggestions about how to deal with your "what if" fears? The way to let go of such fears is to acknowledge God's presence, God's power, and God's love. When you and I think "what if…" questions, we fail to acknowledge God. That's when we need to turn to His Word and be reminded of the many promises that God is with us wherever we go (Joshua 1:9).

And remember this, too: Your God is the God of the past, the present, *and* the future! He has promised to guide you throughout your life and receive you to glory afterward (Psalm 73:24). You can shout along with David that "surely goodness and mercy shall follow me all the days of my life; and I will dwell in the house of the LORD forever" (Psalm 23:6).

Noting a Few "Nothings"

I hope you are getting excited! These truths mean we experience peace instead of worry when we choose to believe the Bible's promises that God will superintend every future event. Therefore…

- *Nothing* will ever happen to you that God does not already know about (Psalm 139:1-4).

- *Nothing* will ever happen to you that is a mistake (Psalm 139:4,16).

- *Nothing* will ever happen that you cannot handle by God's power and grace (2 Corinthians 12:9-10).

- *Nothing* will ever happen to you that will not eventually be used by God for some good purpose in your life (Romans 8:28).

- *Nothing* will ever happen to you without God's presence (Matthew 28:20).

Loving God...Even More

*B*eloved, with promises like these, how can we not but love God? So how can you love God...even more? By remembering that the future is not real. The future exists only in the imagination. Then, when the future arrives... whether in the next minute, hour, or tomorrow...you will —and, by God's grace, you can!—deal with it then, when it is truly present and real. Plan for the future and set goals for yourself, but also be sure to leave them in God's hands. Use your energy to draw close to God in the present and to train your thoughts to think about and deal with things that are true and real...right now!

(P.S. Here's another "nothing" for you as you love God with all your mind: *Nothing* will ever separate you from God's love—Romans 8:38-39!)

$\mathscr{T}$HINKING THE TRUTH ABOUT...THE PAST AND THE PRESENT

∽◈∾

*Fix your thoughts on what is true
and honorable and right.*

PHILIPPIANS 4:8 NLT

$\mathscr{O}$NE OF MY PASSIONS IS READING the biographies of missionaries. These full-of-faith saints teach me much about living a life of faith and endurance. One such person was Adoniram Judson (1788–1850), who has emerged as a personal favorite. This missionary to Burma suffered opposition, failed health, imprisonment, hardship, deprivation, and the death of his wife...and all of this suffering occurred within the first 13 years of his 30-plus years of ministry! Yet this was the man who declared, "The future is as bright as the promises of God."

What a lifestyle! Can't you just relish the power of waking up each day to what is true and real, and staring it in the eye with an attitude of heart and mind that knows that

the future is as bright as the promises of God? What a spectacular way to face the future, no matter how trying—
thinking on the truths about God and His promises from
His Word!

But what about the past? How are you and I to deal
with it? And the present? What will help us cope with
reality, with the way things really are?

Thinking About the Past

Like our "what if" thoughts about the future, "if only"
thoughts about the past can rob us of peace and joy in the
present. And the exhortation in Philippians 4:8—to think on
"whatever things are true [or real]"—comes to our rescue
concerning our thoughts about the past. That's because the
past is no more real than the future.

A personal story—I know firsthand how tightly we can
be gripped by the habit of looking to events in the past and
thinking, "If only I had done that differently....If only I hadn't
done that....If only that hadn't happened....If only I had
been better informed." Here's just one example of my
problems with the past.

For years after I became a Christian, I struggled with the
thought, "If only I had become a Christian sooner!" After
all, I reasoned, coming to Christ sooner would have given
Jim and me God's guidelines for our marriage and for
raising our two daughters. The eight years of marriage
before I knew Christ were rough ones. And adding two
children hadn't helped! However, when Christ entered our
hearts and our home and we began to read God's Word,
His Spirit opened our eyes and showed us how to live
God's way. It was then I realized I had missed out on some

precious opportunities and some important years of nurturing my daughters because I was focusing on myself. So
my heart cried out, "If only I had become a Christian
sooner, I would have been a better wife and mother, I
would have had Christ's love to share in our home, I would
have known to serve and sacrifice instead of being so
selfish! If only…"

Finally the Holy Spirit pointed me to the truth that God
was in complete, sovereign control of my salvation and my
life! It was as if He asked me, "Elizabeth, who was in
charge of your salvation? Who picked the exact day and
minute? Who knew from before time began when you
would believe in Jesus? Who knew about the two little girls
and their needs? Who handpicked you to be their mother?
Who used a rocky marriage and an unfulfilling family life
to open your eyes to your needs?"

At this point, I was on my knees in adoration of God,
the One who controlled my life in the past and controls it
in the present and into the future! *He* knew how my life
would unfold. *He* knew when I would come to know Him.
He knew how I would come to serve Him. This is what is
true and real and far more important than my "if only"
moanings and mournings.

And I'm not alone…

Jenny's story — Jenny, a woman I sat next to at a seminary wives' luncheon, also struggled with "if only" thinking.
As the women at the luncheon told how their husbands
had come to attend seminary, a common thread in many of
the stories was meeting and marrying in college. Jenny, the
last one to share, lamented, "I feel left out here today. If
only I had gone to college…."

Next on the agenda was my time to teach about (guess what!) thinking on what is real instead of on "if only's." When I finished and sat down, Jenny smiled, leaned over, and whispered, "Thanks so much! I really needed that. I'll never say 'if only' again."

But think about Jenny's situation. What was true and real about it? Was God able to direct Jenny's past and bring her and her husband together even though they both didn't go to college? And could God use Jenny mightily even though she didn't have a college education? I think you know the answer, right? *Of course!* These facts are what was true and real! Jenny's "if only" thinking was unnecessary and untrue. And it was holding her back by fostering feelings of inferiority and regret.

Remembering to Think on What Is True

Note it well: "If only" thinking is counterproductive. How is that? Because it doesn't address what is real. The past is gone. It is beyond repair, beyond restructuring. What is real is what is happening today. And God calls us to deal with what is now, what is true, and what is real.

And, as we've seen in Jenny...and perhaps as you yourself have experienced, "if only" thinking breeds remorse. The backward gaze can produce regret and sorrow because it is impossible to return to the past or change the past. So we must ask, What value is there in rehashing it?

Remembering two exceptions—But also note these exceptions: It is good to remember what we've learned from our mistakes. Those lessons are pearls of wisdom. And it is also good to recall God's marvelous works and gracious faithfulness to us. We should look back and remember how

God enabled us in our times of need. Our faith in God is strengthened when we recall how God brought us through our trials, how He taught us on the mountains and in the valleys of life. Psalm 77, often referred to as a "cure for depression,"[1] says we are to meditate on God's goodness in the past whenever the trials of the present seem overwhelming. At such a time, the poet declared, "I will *remember* the works of the LORD; surely I will *remember* Your wonders of old" (verse 11).

So go ahead. Look back at the past…but do so with an eye to appreciate God's faithfulness!

Remembering facts about God—Here's something else to note. When you succumb to "if only" thinking, you fail to acknowledge God's role in your past. You are ignoring the fact that God was there with you. He was with you then…just as He is with you today…and will be with you tomorrow (Psalm 73:23-24).

When you acknowledge God by remembering the facts and evidence of about His care and His character, the wondrous truths about Him help you look back without regret or remorse through eyes of faith.

Looking Back Through Eyes of Faith

Do you know happens when you and I look back at the past without trusting that God was there with us and concerned about us? We sentence ourselves to a life of regret.

Trusting God's guidance—That is what one missionary couple Jim and I met seemed to be doing. When it was time for their oldest child to start school, they enrolled her in a Christian boarding school. At the end of that first year, the little girl told her parents about her year of loneliness and tears. At that moment, they concluded that they had made a horrible mistake.

My wise Jim listened to their story and then asked, "Did you pray before you decided to send your daughter to boarding school?" Devoted Christians and devoted parents, they had indeed prayed.

Jim then asked, "Did you seek wise counsel before you decided to send her to boarding school?" Again, the answer was a hearty yes.

Gently, Jim asked, "Do you think that after you prayed and sought wise counsel, your decision really could have been a horrible mistake?"

What joy it was for us to watch their faces as, for the first time, this hurting couple looked back at their experience through the eyes of faith! Their "if only" thinking was keeping them from remembering their prayerful, biblical decision-making process. A burden was lifted from the shoulders of our new friends and God's servants! They found real relief as they recalled how they had sought God's guidance each step of the way. As hard as that year must have been on their daughter, they could trust that God had been present with her and that He would use that hard time for her good.

Trusting God's overruling power—Here's something else that's true and real about God. As the God of the past, our heavenly Father does indeed *use* our past. The great truth of Romans 8:28-29 is God's promise that any and all "negative" events in the past will be "overruled" and worked for good to make you more like Christ. By His transforming power, God will redeem even the worst, the most painful, and the most perplexing aspects of your past.

I've seen God redeem the suffering and the terrible trials in many people's lives, and I'm sure you have, too. In fact, some of the saints I know who graciously and continually extend God's gentleness, peace, and encouragement to others are those who have tasted pain. God, in His goodness and power, has used their experiences to make them more Christlike, and He is truly glorified in their lives.

Thinking About the Present

And what about the present? Just as we need to follow the exhortation of Philippians 4:8 when thinking about the future ("What if...?") and the past ("If only..."), we need to think on what is true and real in the present. Believe me, I know this is not always easy to do! Too often we are tempted to say, "But this isn't the way it was supposed to be."

A personal story—As a young mother, I chose Proverbs 22:6 as a guiding scripture for raising my children. This admonition says parents are to "train a child in the way he should go, and when he is old he will not depart from it." Holding tightly to this promise, I began to train my children in the way they "should go." A decade later, however, my parenting didn't seem to be working the way I wanted it to. I wasn't reaping the results I had expected. Angry, I said to God, "But this isn't the way it was supposed to be! This isn't the way it went for this family here or that family over there. And this isn't the way it was supposed to be for my family!"

Like a little girl who doesn't get what she wants, I threw a spiritual tantrum. I used my time and energy kicking, screaming, and battling God. Then one day, when I finally took a breath during my rantings to listen, God seemed to say, "But, Elizabeth, this is the way it really is. Now what are you going to do about the way it really is?" I realized I had to quit yelling (so to speak), get up, and go on. And I did.

I was *forced* to face reality. You see, because of my unmet expectations I was postponing any action. Because I didn't like what I saw (which was real!), I was failing to do anything to try to improve the situation. I neglected to deal with the circumstances. Furthermore, I wasn't prepared to because "this wasn't the way it was supposed to be!" And as long as I had that attitude—as long as I didn't accept reality—no progress or solution was possible. As long as I wished for reality to be different, I failed to handle the problem, which was quite real!

Other people struggle, too — I know many women who refuse to face reality when it comes to their marriages. It seems that our fantasies, expectations, and dreams about what marriage will be are usually quite different from the truth. Then, when reality sets in, many women are too stunned and confused to do anything about it. Unhappy, they say to me, "I don't know why I ever married my husband in the first place. I wish I hadn't. This isn't the way it was supposed to be!"

Then, as a friend, I must be the one to say, oh so gently, "But this is the way it really is. Now, what are you going to do about the way it is?" Then the two of us get to work on a solution, a remedy, a plan. You see, once we accept reality—the reality of the condition of our marriage, our family, our job, whatever—we can then use our time and energy to make that reality better.

Loving God…Even More

*A*nd now it's your turn. I've shared some of my personal struggles, and I've shared instances from the lives of others. But the most important person reading this book is you.

What does your past hold? What people, events, and circumstances from days gone by have caused you difficulties or brought problems into your life? You love God with all your mind when you acknowledge His sovereignty over every event of your life—past and present, as well as future.

Think about it this way. Whatever has happened to you in days gone by, the Bible teaches us that, as the supreme and sovereign ruler and the One who is omnipresent through time, God knew the events of your life…before the foundation of the world (2 Timothy 1:9). He knew each detail of the path your life would take. He has allowed your life to unfold as it has. He has overseen all that has happened to you. He has been present with you every step and second along the way. And He has been involved in your life as His plan for you has unfolded.

In short, God is the author and the finisher of your faith *and* your life (Hebrews 12:2)! He is the God of not only your future and your present…but also of your past.

Here's an assignment for you: The next time you catch yourself saying or thinking "if only," first, just stop. Ponder the fact of God's sovereignty, knowledge, and presence in any and all past situations. Refuse to allow yourself to get bogged down thinking about something that is no longer real. Instead, thank God for His continual presence with

you throughout time and for His promise—and power!—
to overrule and redeem the hard times of the past.

And what about the present? About the way things really
are for you today? Your assignment here is to accept what
is real and acknowledge again that God oversees and has
overseen every detail of your life—your singleness, your
marriage, your family, your relationships, your job, your
every situation and your every circumstance. This knowledge will help you to act on what is true and real
today...rather than resent reality and idly wait for fantasies
to magically materialize.

Beloved, with a heart full of faith and hope, with God
by your side, and by His great grace, you can love
Him...even more, no matter what has—or is—happening
to you.

6

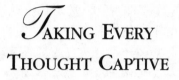

_T_AKING EVERY
THOUGHT CAPTIVE

⌒∞⌒

*All that rings true...let this be
the argument of your thoughts.*

PHILIPPIANS 4:8 KNOX BIBLE

*I*F YOU'RE LIKE ME, RIGHT ABOUT NOW you're wondering, "How can I cultivate the kind of thinking that leads to loving God with all my mind?" That was my heart's cry as I began to wrestle with the challenge to think on what is true and real.

Two decades have passed since my breakthrough occurred as a result of tapping into Philippians 4:8. As a result, I can tell you three steps that have helped me and many others develop thought patterns based on God's truth —thought patterns that enable us to love Him even more. Following these steps will definitely move you forward in training your thoughts.

Step 1: Recognizing the Command

Consider again the apostle Paul's final words in Philippians 4:8: "Meditate on these things." Here Paul issues a command to us to think on what is true and real. He is not making a suggestion, and he's not offering a piece of advice that we can take or leave. No, Philippians 4:8 is God's *command* to us to focus our thoughts on the truth of His Word and on the things in life that are real.

So how can we obey this command from Scripture? Here's how I began. Right away it helped me to realize that it is sin to not obey this command. I didn't want to sin, and I'm sure you don't either. So I reasoned, "If the Bible says I should think only on what is true and real, then to think outside of these biblical boundaries is sin."

Wow! I certainly had my "work" (so to speak!) cut out for me. Labeling thoughts that are not based on what is true or real as "sin" was a powerful daily motivator. And the same is still true today. If I want my thoughts to measure up to God's standard of true and real, then I have to accept that my thinking is either based on God's truth or it isn't. My thinking is either right or wrong. It's either acceptable or sinful. I feel that I have to be this rigid if I am to give up of my destructive thought patterns and obey God by thinking on what is true and real.

Are you baffled as to how in the world you are going to be able to obey God's command? Well, take heart, my friend! You have help! God, by and through His grace, is at work helping you (and me!) accomplish all that He calls you to do. Put another way, it is *He* who enables you to love Him with your whole mind.

Step 2: Responding in Obedience

Next, I began asking, "How can I limit my thinking to what is true and real?" Soon I found a clue from Paul himself in 2 Corinthians 10:4-5. Here he writes,

> For the weapons of our warfare are...mighty in God for pulling down strongholds, casting down arguments and every high thing that exalts itself against the knowledge of God, bringing every thought into captivity to the obedience of Christ.

By definition, thoughts that are not true or real are mere "arguments" or, as the New American Standard Bible says, "speculations." They are not truth. They are "high things" raised up against the knowledge of God and the truth of His Word. And such "things" and thoughts have to be brought "into captivity to the obedience of Christ."

As I considered what "bringing every thought into captivity to the obedience of Christ" means, I immediately thought of something from my childhood. While growing up in a tiny Oklahoma town (population 2,000), it was a grand occasion each year when our family attended the local rodeo. And the calf roping was my favorite event.

Here's the scene—The cowboy, ready on his horse, with lasso in hand, waited for a calf to be released from its chute. Then came the chase as the cowboy raced his horse after the bucking, twisting, running animal, lassoed it, brought it in, jumped off his horse, threw the calf down, tied three legs together, stood up, and raised his hands in victory. The timer stopped, and everyone cheered. The cowboy had successfully roped the calf!

It hit me that to handle my thoughts that were not true or real, I needed to be like that cowboy! You see, my inaccurate thoughts about God and His Word—along with my "what if," "if only," and "this isn't the way it was supposed to be" thoughts—were like that calf! They were untamed and rebellious, bucking, jumping, and running wild in my mind.

So, like the cowboy—and with God's strength and help!—I needed to chase after my wrong thoughts, rope them, bring them in, throw them down, and tie them up. That's how I could experience a victory in my thought-life.

Taking our thoughts captive to Christ—to the Word of God, to what is true and real—calls for energy, effort, and a heart commitment to obey God. It is a battle—a battle fought *in* the mind and a battle *for* the mind. And it is a battle fought one thought at a time...for victory over one thought at a time. It is warfare! And the truth of Philippians 4:8 is a weapon we simply must have in our arsenal. Praise God, this is a battle we can fight—and win!—by His grace.

Step 3: Reaping the Benefits

And now for the glorious blessings! What are some of the fantastic benefits you and I enjoy when we obey God's command to think on what is true and real? When we begin "bringing every thought into captivity to the obedience of Christ"? Here's a short list of what we will experience.

- Greater love for God as we think on what He has done for us

- Exceeding joy from pleasing God through obedience

- Positive well-being from living the way God wants us to live

- Improved relationships with others

- Less stress and more peace in our daily lives

- Accelerated spiritual growth and maturity

Energy for God's purposes— But there is one other benefit that every person I know needs and desires, and that is greater energy! Greater spiritual energy, physical energy, mental energy, and emotional energy—greater energy of every kind for handling life's demands, challenges, and opportunities. It's amazing that as we spend less time in melancholy introspection and more time thinking thoughts that are true and real, we have more energy for positive uses and constructive purposes.

I know I experience this multiplication of energy, and I also see it in others. For instance, in my ministry to seminary wives in Southern California, I saw it in the women I met who, new to California, spent their energy thinking about where they used to live, which was no longer true or real. The result? They felt bad, sad, and bitter about where they did live.

Also, many people I meet waste time reminiscing about the good ol' days (which are no longer true and real), and let today (which is true and real) slip right by them. Others are consumed by thoughts of where they wish they were, what they want to have, what could have been, or what they might have done. When we choose this kind of thinking, real life passes by, unused and unenjoyed. My friend, futile thoughts like these drain our precious energy. It is wasted on what is false and what is fantasy. It is spent on all the wrong things—on what are mere memories and speculations!

Strength for today's issues—For a moment, think of your Christian life as a bucket that God wants to fill so that you can enjoy Him and enjoy life. He wants to fill your life with Himself so He can use it to glorify Him, to bless you, and to enrich the lives of others.

Now, how do you fill the bucket with the things of God? Reading the Bible every day is one way. You can also memorize and meditate on Scripture. And you can pray and worship. But you must also realize that every wrong thought you think—thoughts that are not true and real—is like a hole in your spiritual bucket. Every time you think inaccurately about God, about God's Word, and about people, you are draining your bucket. Every time you dwell on "what if" and "if only" and "this isn't the way it was supposed to be" scenarios, you can be sure your energy is leaking out!

My friend, it's a fact: Thinking about things that are untrue and unreal drain your energy, your life, and your strength for dealing with today's issues! Obeying the command of Philippians 4:8, however, helps keep your bucket filled and overflowing! and your energy available to serve God, to take care of your responsibilities, and to move toward accomplishing your dreams.

Loving God...Even More _____

$\mathcal{D}$o you remember how this book started? With me answering the phone call regarding my struggles with depression. Well, dear friend, that call forced me to recognize how God's Word helped me conquer that horrendous daily problem. And, I have to report, that look back strengthened my commitment to know even more of God's truth and to do exactly what it says!

As I remember the kind of woman I was and the kind of life I lived due to the thoughts that filled my head, I am astonished. Having been a prisoner of dark moods generated by dark thoughts, I know all too well the frightening ability our thoughts have to program our lives. Scripture's analysis is true: "As [a person] thinks in his heart, so he is" (Proverbs 23:7).

As I look back, I am also overwhelmed with gratitude to God for His wisdom. Knowing the struggles His people would have, He provided help for us through the Bible, His written, inspired, profitable, living, powerful, and sharper-than-any-two-edged-sword Word (2 Timothy 3:16; Hebrews 4:12)! As we have seen, when the apostle Paul calls us in Philippians 4:8 to meditate on what is true and real, he is giving us what one commentator labeled a "paragraph on mental health."[1] How thankful I am that God gave me fresh insight into Philippians 4:8 when I needed it so desperately!

Paul gave Philippians 4:8 to help the church at Philippi deal with its problems. And, beloved, this scripture contains truth that also helps you and me develop a healthier thought-life and enjoy the peace of mind, energy, and effectiveness that come when we love God with all our mind.

My prayer for you, dear friend—and for myself—is that we will...

—love God *more* and
   —experience *more* of His love
      —by knowing *more* of His Word and
         —by submitting *more* of our life to His truth.

Winning over Worry

❦

Do not worry about tomorrow,
for tomorrow will worry about
its own things. Sufficient for
the day is its own trouble.

Matthew 6:34

7

*F*OCUSING ON TODAY

❦

Do not worry about tomorrow,
for tomorrow will worry about
its own things. Sufficient for
the day is its own trouble.

MATTHEW 6:34

*H*OW DO THE FIRST MINUTES of your days usually go? Are they anything like mine used to be? Here's a typical scenario from the past, from the days before I learned to think on what is true and real.

Looking at All of Life

The first sound I heard was the blaring alarm clock. Despite the fog of disturbed sleep, I managed to hit the snooze button. I slept deeply through the first nine-minute interval. However, during the next snooze period, my mind moved quickly from barely functioning...to worrying...to a full panic.

"Oh, no!" I moaned. "Another day! Another thousand things to do." And sure enough, the panic had begun. I knew that my bright, fresh day was a gift from God. And, oh how I wanted to say with the psalmist, "This is the day the LORD has made; we will rejoice and be glad in it" (Psalm 118:24). But I just couldn't. I was too overwhelmed by the mountain range of responsibility that comprised my life. My list was long, my schedule was full, and my calendar was booked. Doing all I needed to do that day seemed impossible. And I wasn't even out of bed yet! People, commitments, deadlines, work, housework, errands, needs—my list was endless.

And I'll bet your list and life probably look—and feel!—a lot like mine did. Yes, we know all too well that life is crowded, complex, and challenging. There is always soooo much to do!

Looking at God's Word

But in Matthew 6:34, God's Word comes to our rescue. God gives us His view on the days of our lives and His surefire instructions for handling the "trouble" and trials that come with each one of them. He gives us His truth to think on, believe in, and act on—truth that is true and real, truth that will help us win over worry. Hear now as Jesus speaks to the too-common feeling of being overwhelmed by life. He says to you and to me,

> Do not worry about tomorrow, for tomorrow will
> worry about its own things. Sufficient for the day
> is its own trouble.

Looking at Today

With these words of commonsense wisdom, Jesus reduces our responsibilities to those of today...and today only. He forces our focus from the panorama view of the mountain range of all our tomorrows...to the single mountain of today. You see, today is all Christ asks us to cope with. And today is something Christ knows we—with His help—can indeed manage. His words give us hope, and they give us focus. Matthew 6:34 includes Christ's formula for winning over worry. It consists of...

His command—
> *Do not worry about tomorrow,*

His insight—
> *Tomorrow will worry about its own things,* and

His challenge for us today—
> *Sufficient for the day is its own trouble.*

Dear friend, Jesus calls us away from worrying about tomorrow (a major contributor to stress) and to addressing the reality of today. His job assignment for us can be boiled down to three words: "Deal with today!"

The five very practical guidelines presented in the next few chapters have helped me obey Christ's command, adopt His insights, and accept His challenge to focus on today. With that focus, I am more able to love God with all my mind...even as I go about meeting the practical, nuts-and-bolts demands of the day.

As you read through this section on "Winning over Worry," you will see how these same steps will also enable you to meet each day's emotional, physical, and mental demands as well.

Guideline 1: Prepare

Prepare in the evening—If you were going to climb a mountain early tomorrow morning, I'm sure you would do certain tasks the night before. Well, the same is true for everyone who feels overwhelmed by the demands on them. They do well to follow this same principle of doing certain tasks the night before. For instance...

Look at tomorrow's calendar. What is scheduled? What's happening at work? What's going on in each family member's life?

And by the way, What's planned for dinner? If this is your responsibility, you can prepare as much of tomorrow's evening meal as possible (make the Jell-O, cook the potatoes for potato salad, thaw the chicken pieces, wash and tear the lettuce, chop the vegetables, assemble the casserole). And while you're in the kitchen, go ahead and prepare tomorrow's lunches and set the table for the next meal. Clean up the kitchen and run the dishwasher. Nothing starts a day better than an orderly kitchen.

Before you go to bed, take a few minutes to organize and pick things up, to tidy your space. Again, your neatness and efforts will be a blessing in the morning. Also, lay out clothes for tomorrow so you won't have to think about what to wear in the morning. Before you turn out the lights, put everything you'll need for tomorrow (lunches, briefcases, the dry cleaning, schoolbags, coats, purse, keys, cell phones, mail, packages...you know the list!) by the door. Then, as you go to bed, be sure the alarm is set at a time that ensures that you have enough time to do what needs to be done in the morning...in a calm, orderly manner.

Now, you're half ready to climb that mountain of tomorrow!

Prepare in the morning—The first step we take each new day is crucial because it sets the tone for the day. I've found that getting up when the alarm goes off (versus hitting the snooze button too many times!) puts me in control of my day. (How about you?)

Then, once we're up, we need spiritual input for the day. Jesus knew the value of an early-morning meeting with the Father. In Mark 1:35, we learn that "in the morning, having risen a long while before daylight ['while it was still dark' NASB], He went out and departed to a solitary place; and there He prayed." A little background information makes this feat even more startling. You see, the day before, Jesus had spent His time and energy preaching, casting out demons, and healing many people. Even after sundown, He "healed many who were sick with various diseases, and cast out many demons" (verse 34). Nevertheless, the next morning, after a full and challenging—and successful in human terms—day, Jesus rose early to spend time in prayer so He would be refreshed and refilled for another day of ministry.

However (and I'm sure you can relate!), Jesus' time alone with God was interrupted. Simon Peter and his friends approached Him, saying, "Everyone is looking for You" (verse 37).

Stop just a minute, please. Do you ever feel as if everyone is looking for you? That everyone needs something from you? With people depending on you, you probably have very few moments alone, and even then you know that you're "on call." Our Jesus knows what it's like to have people clamoring after Him for what only He can give. But as one writer points out, although "Christ's life was surrounded by hurricane-like winds and forces...they never deterred Him from His priorities or His sense of mission! He was never unnerved and never responded in a way that was out of line with His character."[1] Jesus remained focused in His work and was loving toward people because He spent time with His Father, "a time of restorative withdrawal... [where] energies are renewed, perspectives refocused, and directions newly defined."[2]

If you're like me, you may find that your most harried days are those days when you have failed to make time to be with Christ. When we "put Christ off, the result is frequently exhaustion (both physical and spiritual), loss of perspective, defensiveness, self-pity, and an absence of joy....We become sapped. With [Christ] we seem tireless by contrast."[3]

Is that your experience? Like Jesus shows us, we must first withdraw from the people who need us so that we will be able to serve them later. When we are faithful to take this all-important step of preparation, we will be more ready to give to others because we will have already received from the Father the guidance, perspective, strength, and grace we need for the day.

Now back to Mark, chapter 1. When the disciples found Jesus and told Him "Everyone is looking for You," Christ confidently said, "Let us go into the next towns, that I may preach there also, because for this purpose I have come forth" (verse 38).

Where did this come from? After all, hadn't Jesus just experienced a tremendously—and miraculously!—"successful" day of ministry there in Capernaum? Shouldn't He remain there and continue to repeat what was obviously working? No. Jesus had obtained fresh orders for His fresh new day in His early morning time with the Father. Furthermore, following the Father's plan took priority over the seemingly urgent needs of the crowds who were looking for Him.

There's a loud lesson here for you and me. We, who so easily fall into the trap of other people's plans for us or give in to "the tyranny of the urgent" without a second thought, can learn from Christ's example. In His quiet time alone with God, before the sun rose, in the stillness of time before daybreak, Jesus focused on the new day. And He let that focus shape His plans for the day. When we don't take time to be alone with God, you and I endanger our relationship with God, our health, and our service to others. In fact, "without large blocks of silence and solitude…we are in danger of losing the very best things that people desire to draw from us."[4]

By contrast, alone with God, during some hushed moments (which are quite different from the hurry and scurry of the rushed activities and busyness of the rest of the day!), we receive from God what people will need us to give to them during the day ahead. Then, by the time everyone is looking for us, by the time the family gets up, the phone rings, or we get into the car, we have God's direction for our day.

Loving God…Even More

What happens when you take time to prepare—spiritually and practically—for each day's mountain climb, when you properly gear up for stepping into the day ahead of you? The list of benefits is long, but here are two you'll notice right away.

Your list of blessings begins with *God's love*. You are more aware of receiving God's love throughout the day when right from the start of each brand-new day your mind is focused on Him and His daily assignment to you. It's *His* day—the day the *Lord* has made. And He has lovingly given the day to you for enjoying Him, glorifying Him, loving Him, and serving Him and the people He chooses to put in your path.

And here's another blessing: *God's perspective*. Taking time alone with God to obtain His perspective on your responsibilities and His ordering of your day's activities will enable you to climb the mountain of today. When you start the day reminded of God's love and focused on His purposes for you, you are better prepared to meet the challenges ahead, including the challenge of loving God through each and every second.

Amazingly, when you make time alone with God your first priority for each day, you begin to live out the command of Matthew 6:33—

> *Seek first the kingdom of God*
> *and His righteousness.*

And then you begin to realize the promise of Matthew 6:33, the promise of God's provision of all that you need...the truth that makes it possible for you to win over worry—

> *and all these things*
> *shall be added to you.*

8

$\mathcal{S}$CALING THE MOUNTAIN
OF TODAY

᪳

Do not worry about tomorrow;
for tomorrow will care for itself.
Each day has enough trouble of its own.

MATTHEW 6:34 NASB

$\mathcal{D}$O YOU TEND TO WORRY ABOUT getting through the work, handling the responsibilities, and meeting head-on the challenges that seem to arrive with each new day? Then you, dear friend and reader—and fellow worrier!—should memorize Matthew 6:34. This powerful worry-buster is part of Christ's famous Sermon on the Mount. Kingdom living on earth is His topic, and verse 34 falls into His calling of Christians away from worry about tomorrow—a key cause of tension—and back to the reality of dealing with today. This God-breathed verse is divine help for worrywarts. It is God's truth, shot straight from His heart to yours! To win over worry, you (and all believers) must simply think on this verse and put it to use throughout today...and all the days of your life.

So far we know that to heed Christ's command in Matthew 6:34 to "not worry about tomorrow," we must tend to first things first. We need to follow *Guideline 1* and *prepare* for each new day—practically the night before, and spiritually the morning of (see chapter 7). Then we must move on to...

Guideline 2: Plan Ahead

Like preparing, planning—both long-range and short-range—enables us to follow Christ's instructions for winning over worry. It also makes us more effective during our day.

Long-range planning—Breaking large projects into day-sized bits and pieces is an exercise that keeps us from feeling overwhelmed by our goals and our work. And it also fixes our focus on today. For instance, long-range planning is key to birthday and anniversary celebrations, weddings, reunions, parties, vacations, and business or pleasure trips. Presentations, papers, articles, and dissertations require the same long-range planning that redecorating, adding on to your house, or building a new one demands. We also need to plan ahead for buying or selling a home. And then there's planning for retirement.

I first learned about long-range planning in my own living room where Jim and I were trying to hang new wallpaper. We had the paper and the equipment we needed, but we didn't have a weekend or even a single open day to do the job. Overwhelmed, I stood in the middle of the living room and sobbed, "We'll never get this done. We just don't have time to do this. We'll just get all the stuff out, make a big mess, and then we'll have to put it all away. There's no way to get this done!"

These 30 years later I still remember Jim's next words— "Honey, how do you eat an elephant?" After I whimpered, "I don't know," Jim said, "You eat an elephant one bite at a time. We're going to get the stuff out, we're going to cut the first strip, we're going to put it on the wall, and then we'll put it all away...but we will have taken the first bite." And then we put this "elephant-eating principle" to work. We took the first "bite" and made some progress!

As you can see, long-range planning breaks large projects into small tasks. Such forward thinking enables us to obey Christ's command to not be anxious for tomorrow. Instead of worrying, we can deal with the future by bringing manageable pieces—bites, if you will—into the present day's tasks. This reduces the waste of precious time and energy on worry, fear, panic, or dread of the future. With planning, we are more likely to meet life's challenges head-on and reach our life goals.

Short-term planning—This helps us to meet the day's demands. For me, lists are key. Every morning I make a "to do" list of my work tasks for the day at hand. Included on my daily to-do list are "bites" from my long-range projects, as well as those day-to-day items that are part of keeping a busy life going. The list tells me *what* I need to do. Then, once I complete my list, I schedule *when* I will do each job. Lists and a schedule help me get the work done—the work of today and "its own trouble," and the work of the future that causes me to worry if I'm not doing something (even a small something) about it.

My friend Janelle told me how lists helped her deal with an especially stressful time in her life. She was expecting a baby any time, remodeling her house, and fighting the cleaning problems the construction created. Her solution? Planning! She explained,

> I sat down and wrote out all the projects under three headings—Baby, Remodel, and General Cleaning. I have been able to plan each day by selecting one or two things from each heading to get done that day. This has helped immensely. Instead of one huge to-do list that I know will never get done before the baby arrives, I've been able to put things into manageable bites—and by God's grace, I'm making headway!

Having a plan—a schedule—and Matthew 6:34 to remind you not to be anxious can help you design a productive, enjoyable day that's free of frustration and anxiety and their effects on your life...not to mention, a day characterized by closeness with the Lord!

Guideline 3: Pray

As we prepare and plan, we must also pray, pray, pray! Each day, I try to make the following three transactions a part of my prayers.

First, I *give God everything*. I begin by giving Him myself. British preacher and writer F. B. Meyer had seven rules to live by every day, and Number One on his list was "make a daily, definite, audible consecration of yourself to God. Say it out loud: Lord, today I give myself anew to you."[1] When I give myself to God like this, it reminds me that as His child I belong to Him. And, as a bookmarker in my Bible says, "God is ready to assume full responsibility for the life wholly yielded to Him."

I also *give God the things in my life*—my home, my possessions, my time, my body, and my mind. This prayerful commitment reminds me again that God has given me everything I have, and I am to care for them and use them in ways that honor and please Him.

I *give God the people in my life*—my husband, my children and their spouses, my grandchildren, and my family members. My love is fierce when it comes to these precious people! But giving them to God calms my thoughts and quiets my worries. He is all-wise, all-powerful, loving, and able to take care of the things *and* the people in our lives.

Peace of mind is available to you, too, when you give God everything—yourself, your things, and the people you care about—as well as the physical, practical, and emotional concerns of your life. All these are His to do with as He likes! This complete commitment to God of all that you are and all that you have is another way you love Him with all your mind—and making this commitment daily is key.

Second, after giving God everything, I *give God my Plan A for the day*. Giving Him my schedule for the day— correction: *His* day!—means laying before Him the projects I want to get done and think I must get done. Committing my plans to God helps me fight against impulsiveness and laziness. It also helps me to follow Him if He leads me in a new direction.

Third (and this is crucial!), I *give God Plan B for the day.* Although I have a plan—Plan A—I want God's will for my life. Therefore I commit my day, my goals, my time, and my energies to Him. I pray to hold my Plan A loosely and to yield to Him during the course of the day. You see, I want my plan to be *His* plan. So, if and when God moves me to do something different—Plan B, *His* plan—I want to be ready, willing, and available.

The perspective that comes with surrendering my agenda to God reduces my frustration. I make Plan A and submit it to God. But when I give Him Plan B, I am acknowledging His right to alter my day. My thinking then goes like this: "Plan A is good...unless God moves me to Plan B. Then 'Plan B is better' because Plan B is God's plan." Knowing God is behind any and every unexpected event helps me accept whatever happens. Besides reducing my frustration level when my plans change, giving God Plan B helps me be more flexible. Writer and pastor Ray Ortlund explains:

> I like to start out the morning covering my whole day by prayer....I take out my appointment book and pray through the hours. I pray for everyone I am scheduled to see....I pray for the unscheduled ones I will bump into. I've found that if I pray over my interruptions and get them squarely under God's sovereign control, they don't irritate me. I realize that they are part of God's plan.[2]

Again, we are to make a plan for the day, pray over that plan, and then proceed to follow that plan. But we must be willing to accept the unexpected as *God's* intervention, to recognize it as *His* plan...and then flex and flow with it!

And here's another benefit of giving God Plan B—It improves my attitude by leaps and bounds! After committing my day to God, I then say, "Okay, God, let's see what's going to happen! Let's see where this day goes!" This positive outlook gives me an attitude of expectancy and acceptance. I actually look forward to seeing God at work in my life...even though His plan usually proves to be quite different from mine!

Thomas Edison supposedly shouted to his son as his laboratories burned and his life's work was going up in flames, "Son, go get your mother quick! She's never seen a fire like this!" When he and his wife looked over the smoldering ruins the next morning, he said, "Just think. All our mistakes have been burned up, and we have a chance to start all over again."[3] (Oh, Lord, may I have this attitude when my plans seem to be going up in smoke! May I be glad for the chance to do what *You* would have me do.)

Jesus commanded us in Matthew 6:34 to focus on today. And prayer helps us to do just that. Through prayer, we can cast all our anxieties and worries upon God (1 Peter 5:7), give Him everything (including Plan A and Plan B for the day), and experience the peace, focus, wisdom, and strength He gives us for managing the mountain of today. After all, He is the one who enables us to meet Christ's challenge to deal with today's trouble—and today's trouble only!

Guideline 4: Proceed

Preparing, planning, and praying move us to the base of the mountain of today. But finally it is time to actually begin the climb. Ancient wisdom reminds us that "a journey of a thousand miles begins with a single step." And, dear climbing friend, that truth can help us tackle the day one step at a time and one task at a time without worry.

When writing about Jesus' command to put off tomorrow's anxiety until tomorrow, one scholar noted, "If this be done, the greater part of all our anxiety is put aside at once, and for the rest of it, the principle will apply to each hour as well as to each day."[4] In other words, not only do we not need to worry about tomorrow, but we also don't need to worry about the next hour! Why? Because any interruptions and crises are ways God reveals His will for our day. Knowing this frees our concentration and energy to focus on the task at hand. Then, when things change, we'll take the next step and do the next task, again refusing to worry about what lies ahead.

When you prepare, plan, pray, and proceed with a heart that's open to God's plan, you'll find yourself walking with God…with no worries about tomorrow. That's the fruit of obeying the command of Matthew 6:34: *Do not worry about tomorrow.* You can live your day fully. You can experience the joy of the Lord. You can go from task to task, meeting the needs of others. You can do what you must and handle whatever God brings…in His power and without anxiety. And you can wake up tomorrow and do it all over again! As C.S. Lewis wrote, "Relying on God has to begin all over again every day as if nothing yet had been done."[5]

A personal story—Believe it or not, I used to be a runner. And I can't help but think of these steps to winning over worry as being somewhat like my approach to my daily run. Here's the scenario.

I *plan* and *prepare* for my run by first putting on the right clothes and the right shoes (which were laid out the night before). Then I *proceed* out the door. I run to the first major traffic intersection...and then to the next. But as the run gets longer and I get tired, I start targeting the next corner. As I get closer to home, I concentrate on even smaller goals—the next corner, the next trash can on the block, the next driveway, streetlight, or tree. I don't dare look up the huge hill in front of me. I can't! That's too far, too unreachable...but I can take one more step. And I don't dare look all the way home! Again, that's too far...but I can run to the next flower. So, step by step, I complete my run, finally reaching my goal.

Like completing a run, living today begins with preparation, planning, and prayer. But once these things are done, we must then proceed—one step at a time, one task at a time—by focusing our energy on each job as it comes up during the day. This focus helps us to successfully scale the mountain of today and not worry about the mountain of tomorrow. It helps us to live each day to the max!

Guideline 5: Trust God to Provide

There's one more key to winning over worry, and it's a big one — *We must trust God to provide.*

After all of our elaborate preparations and meticulous planning, and after all of our impassioned outpourings in prayer, we must finally proceed. Then, *as* we move forward in faith and obedience to climb the mountain of today, an amazing thing happens. We find that whatever the challenge, task, trial, crisis, or interruption, God provides for us every step of the way! Whatever happens, God provides His wisdom (James 1:5). Whatever happens, God provides His strength (Philippians 4:13; Deuteronomy 33:25; 2 Peter 1:3). Whatever happens, God provides what we need (Philippians 4:19). When we finally move out in faith, we discover that when God commands, He supplies. Where He guides, He provides.

Loving God...Even More

So are you now ready (or more ready) to face your mountain of today? Today will require your full attention and a full-out effort. As Jesus explained, "Sufficient for the day [this day!] is its own trouble." Preparing, planning, praying, and proceeding will enable you to focus on today because these efforts draw you closer to God. And such closeness frees you from the anxiety and worry that keep you from appreciating Him, trusting Him, and loving Him with all your mind.

The five guidelines will also enable you to experience God's provision for you, His beloved child, amid the practical details and demands of daily living. You will experience His provision as He helps you meet the spiritual, mental, physical, and emotional trials of each day.

Dear friend and companion on the climb, proceed ahead! Step out in trust and walk through the days of your life close to the Lord. Not a day will go by without evidence of His care. Not only will you love Him even more, but you will, indeed, win over worry!

9

ℒIVING ONE DAY AT A TIME

❧

Don't worry about tomorrow,
for tomorrow will bring its own worries.
Today's trouble is enough for today.

MATTHEW 6:34 NLT

𝒲HEN THE PERSIAN GULF WAR broke out (1990), I had to learn new applications for Matthew 6:34. The fighting in Kuwait forced me to focus on more than the practicalities of putting meals on the table, providing clean clothes for my family, and being ready to teach Bible classes. I had to learn how to focus on today emotionally. I had to learn how to practice the five principles of preparing, planning, praying, proceeding, and then trusting God to provide when it came to the prospect of my husband going to war!

Reviewing a Slice of History

When Jim and I married, he joined the Army Reserves and, as a registered pharmacist, he was assigned to the Medical Service Corps. After 25 years of routine monthly meetings and after Jim finally qualified for army retirement, we were not prepared for what happened.

In September 1990, Operation Desert Shield began to heat up. The first signs warned that something big was about to happen. Soon the initial escalation of military presence was followed by rumors that reserve units would be called up. Then in October, it happened—Operation Desert Shield became Operation Desert Storm, and that meant war! I still remember holding my breath as President George H. Bush addressed the nation on television and spoke the words our family dreaded. He was authorizing the call-up of reservists!

Gearing up for war—Soon actual call-ups began across the country. Yet at his unit meetings, Jim heard, "There's no way our unit is going to be called. They'll never take us." But just in case, his unit began to prepare for the possibility. The reservists were put on a series of practice alerts, and officers called homes to be sure they could reach their personnel. Next, there were emergency drills and night meetings to ensure the commanding officers could expedite a call-up.

One weekend in October, my husband returned from his monthly drill and reported that the leaders had stopped saying "*if* we go" and were now saying "*when* we go." Unit members spent the next monthly meeting packing for war. And that Thanksgiving our family went away for four days together because Jim had been told he should plan to be in Saudi Arabia...that the military wanted all of its troops in place...before the Christmas holiday.

Soon all of the medical units on the West Coast were in Saudi Arabia except Jim's. His would be next. Then 100 reservists from his unit were activated and an additional 100 were put on alert.

Next word came that Jim, as well as the remainder of his unit, were on official alert. That meant that Jim's duffel bag was packed and by the door, and he was to be within four hours of his unit at all times. Jim was issued a gas mask and trained extensively on how to use it. He was instructed to update his insurance forms and his will and to be sure his family files were in order.

Moving one step closer—One morning while Jim was getting ready to go to work, the phone rang. He was being called up for service in the unit office in downtown Los Angeles for two weeks. And Jim's assignment? To process the soldiers leaving for the war. This decision was made when his superiors discovered that Jim was, at that time, a minister. They decided he would be a perfect replacement for the Family Services officer who had been sent to the Persian Gulf. Jim's job was to support the spouses and families of deployed soldiers.

Suddenly every time our phone rang at home, it was a different woman in tears. "I don't know where my husband is" came the cry. "It's been three weeks, and I haven't heard a word." Finances were another common cause for worry—"He's been gone for two months, and I haven't received his paycheck. What are we going to do without any money?"

The duties of the Family Services officer also included leading support-group meetings for family members left behind. At the meetings, Jim updated them on finances and available services, and he offered children as well as spouses help in coping with depression and anxiety. Often I went along with Jim and, as the people shared their worries and concerns, I joined in their tears. I left those meetings thinking, "This is going to be me next month."

My anguished waiting ended on March 6, 1991, when President Bush announced, "The war is over"...one week before Jim was scheduled to go overseas!

Managing Emotions

Needless to say, the months between October and March were an emotional roller coaster ride for me! Every day I struggled with the emotions that came with not knowing what the future held for Jim and me and our girls. Fear, anxiety, uncertainty—I had to cope with these emotions daily. The practical issues of life—managing schedules, a household, work, and family responsibilities—were challenge enough. But harder for me was managing emotions.

For most of us, our family members are our greatest concern. We worry about our spouses and children, about nurturing our marriage and family relationships, about caring for aging parents. Another emotionally charged area is finances as we worry about layoffs, salary cuts, the rising cost of living, growing families, increasing expenses, the loss of retirement benefits, and a sagging economy. What can we do with these realities that drain our emotions?

As we know from the previous chapter, we can apply Matthew 6:34 to dealing with daily responsibilities and the practicalities of everyday life. And here's more good news! We can also use Christ's truth and guidance for managing the emotions of life. The same directives from our Savior apply: "Do not worry about tomorrow, for tomorrow will worry about its own things. Sufficient for the day is its own trouble." During the Persian Gulf War, anxiety was pressing in on me from every direction, and all I had was this command from Christ. And, beloved, I learned that it was all I needed...because it pointed me to Him. In Matthew 6:34, Jesus commands us not to worry about tomorrow and calls us to handle our emotions...one day at a time. So I applied the same five principles—prepare, plan, pray, proceed, and trust God's provision—to my raging emotions.

We prepared—Jim and I cut our budget. We stopped using credit cards and stopped making major purchases. We also checked into possible jobs for me and did some needed home repairs. Jim talked with the seminary about his employment, salary, and job responsibilities. He met with mortgage company officials about our situation and called the college our two daughters attended to check on their tuition payment policy for activated military parents.

We planned—Jim talked to our daughters at length about what might happen and about what his deployment and even his possible death would mean for them. I put my teaching and speaking engagements on hold, and, pulling together as a family, we took that four-day Thanksgiving vacation.

Jim and I also pulled together as a couple. We discussed every option, every step, every phase, even down to my asking Jim, "What do you want me to do if you don't come back?" Bless him, he anchored me by giving clear and specific instructions for the future.

We prayed—Like never before, Jim and I prayed. I also enlisted the help of "The Faithful Five," a group of long-time praying friends. I phoned each of these women and asked them to pray for me every day, and I called them whenever something happened—an alert, an emergency drill, any news from the army.

In addition to my praying, I fasted. God alone could keep my husband from going to war. There was nothing I could do, and there was nothing Jim could do. There was no human way out. So, I began to fast on December 4. On that first day, I decided that I would fast until I knew Jim was not going to the Persian Gulf or, if he did go, until he came back—or died. That was my covenant with God. I also decided to break my fast each day at sundown, a format that followed the Jewish model and least disrupted our family times...and just happened to correspond to the five o'clock close of all army offices! No phone calls ordering my husband to report to duty in Desert Storm would come after five o'clock!

During this time of praying and fasting, God alone knew of four trials, equal in magnitude to the Persian Gulf War, that I would later face. These trials involved the health of one daughter, cancer biopsies for me, a critical financial crisis, and an extremely difficult relationship with another person. In fact, God used this war to force me into a position of total dependence on Him, which enabled me to better handle those other four situations. In the end, prayer and fasting availed as much for those four situations as for Jim and the 63rd Army Command...and the entire U.S. military!

We proceeded—Besides calling us to prepare and plan, Jesus tells us in Matthew 6:34 how to proceed—"Do not worry about tomorrow." As I went about my daily life, I let this verse set boundaries for my thoughts. I was not to speculate on my future because God wasn't asking me to handle my entire life all at once. Instead, His wisdom was telling me to limit my thoughts to today, to what was real right now. Any "what if" imaginings about the future (as we saw in a previous chapter) were not real. Therefore I didn't need to deal with them. But today was real, and I had to deal with it. As Christ points out, "Sufficient for the day [this day!] is its own trouble."

With God's strength and grace, I would be able to function today. I also knew I wouldn't be able to if I gave in to worrying about tomorrow. So I chose to draw near to God and think on His love for me and His promises to care for me. I chose to love Him with all my mind by attempting to keep my thoughts within His prescribed boundary of today and of what was true and real. Choosing to love God with my mind also helped limit my emotions because, as you and I both know, thoughts generate emotions.

Without God's command to limit my thinking, I don't think I could have emotionally handled all that God asked me to bear during and after the Persian Gulf War. But through the teaching of Matthew 6:34, God was telling me not to feel the emotions that would come in the yet-unrevealed future. "Do not worry" spoke directly to my heart. I let today be the boundary for my concerns and emotions, knowing that tomorrow "would worry about its own things." I proceeded with each day as it came, knowing that God was with me.

Every day, however, seemed like an entire lifetime. Emotionally, physically, and spiritually, I was strained to the limit. Each time the phone rang during these long months, it was bad news. It was Jim's unit, or a distraught spouse, or another doctor's report on my daughter's illness, or more test results concerning my physical problem, or an order for another biopsy. In addition, I was living with my husband as if each day was our last and, at the same time, trying to be sensitive to our children's worries, fears, and needs.

My dear reading friend, peace came only as I followed the wisdom of Matthew 6:34. As I proceeded through those six months, I fought to keep my thoughts and feelings focused to one day at a time. (And I often found myself being a lot like Charlie Brown who glumly reports in one *Peanuts* cartoon, "I used to try to take each day as it came, but my philosophy has changed. I'm down to half a day at a time!")

We experienced God's provision—As I planned, prepared, prayed, proceeded, and lived one day at a time, I saw God provide for me each day. The fact that I am writing about this experience 15 years later is a witness to God's provision for me—to His presence with me and to His work in my life—as I proceeded, by His grace, one day at a time. The final entry in my journal from that time of my life remains a real touchstone for me:

> God, You are so good in Your dealings with me and with my family! Thank You for arranging my life so that I need You so greatly. Thank You for the intimate closeness of my walk with You these past months. Thank You for the humility I feel, the lowliness, the dependency, the brokenness, the cleanness. Thank You for opening the floodgates of my heart for so many others—and at the time of my greatest need! Because You have so adequately met my needs, I can give to others in need. I have needed You and I have sought You, and You have made yourself known to me in

new ways. I know that I have grown in faith. It was tested daily, and I now know You better.

Loving God...Even More

Whenever I look back on that challenging time, I am well aware of the lessons I learned about God and about winning over worry. Did He enable me to deal with the circumstances and the stress? Was His grace sufficient? Did spiritual growth occur in my life? Am I a stronger Christian today because of that experience? Do I know more about my God today? Do I know more about waiting, suffering, trusting, and persevering? Is my faith in God greater? Can I better relate to people's pain? Can I be a more effective minister and servant now? Yes—and a thousand more yeses! My trust in God was tested daily, and the only way to pass those tests was to believe in His atrributes, to walk with Him closely, and to love Him more and more...one day at a time.

10

$\mathcal{L}$IVING OUT OF GOD'S GRACE

&&&

Do not worry about tomorrow,
for tomorrow will worry about itself.
Each day has enough trouble of its own.

Matthew 6:34 niv

$\mathcal{A}$S I FACED MY OWN DAILY STRUGGLE with emotions during the half-year of the Gulf War, I devoured God's word and prayed without ceasing. I also sought to bring my fearful thoughts captive to the obedience of Christ (2 Corinthians 10:5). In addition, I also read biographies describing God's grace to others who had gone before me in their sufferings.

Learning More About Managing Emotions

It was then I found great guidance and wisdom from the writings of missionary Elisabeth Elliot. Sometimes I thought I was silly to feel so much anxiety about my husband's potential service in a war. No, in the end he didn't go overseas. And no, he didn't die. But I only knew that after the fact, so for many months, fear was a daily reality for me. Elisabeth Elliot helped me understand the intensity of my emotions with her observation that "people who have themselves experienced both grief and fear know how alike those two things are....They are equally disabling, distracting and destructive."[1]

Elisabeth Elliot indeed knows about fear and grief. When she was serving in the jungles of Ecuador, she and the other missionary wives received word that two bodies had been found at the location where their husbands had gone. What did she think? How did she feel? What did she do?

Thinking on the truth — First, this missionary wife focused her mind on God and the truth in His Word. "It was the first I knew that anything was amiss," she recalls. "A verse God had impressed on my mind when I first arrived in Ecuador came back suddenly and sharply: 'When thou passest through the waters, I will be with thee, and through the rivers, they shall not overflow thee....' "[2] Armed with this promise of God's presence, she then prayed and proceeded to go about her duties. "I went upstairs to continue teaching the Indian girls' literacy class, praying silently, 'Lord, let not the waters overflow.' "[3]

Jim Elliot was one of the men who was killed. And the way his wife faced this crisis helped me to face mine. I wanted to quit. I felt angry. I wanted to fall down in a heap and cry, focus on myself, and forget about everyone else and their needs! But...

Proceeding ahead—I knew that is not how God wants His people to face a crisis. I had to proceed and press on with my duties and responsibilities. I had to go on living life. And as I did so, I experienced the truth of something else Elisabeth Elliot has written: "At such times I have been wonderfully calmed and strengthened by doing some simple duty...like a bed to be made or a kitchen floor to be washed....Sometimes it takes everything you have to get up and do it, but it is surprising how strength comes."[4]

In times of emotional stress, strength *does* come from routine and responsibility. That's another reason why it's important to have a plan for the day. Life must go on! And we must function! Our families need care, and our homes and lives need order. Doing tasks with these goals in mind keeps us from being immobilized by depression and fear. As Elisabeth Elliot points out, "There is wonderful therapy in getting up and doing something. While you are doing, time passes quickly. Time itself will in some measure heal....And in the doing of whatever comes next, we are shown what to do after that."[5]

And where had Mrs. Elliot, a model of Christian maturity for me, learned how to function when catastrophe struck? Jesus Christ had shown her the way. "Our Lord did not halt all activity to brood over what was to come," she writes. "He was not incapacitated by the fear of suffering, though he well knew that fear. To the question, 'What shall I do?' (so often, for us, the cry of despair) he simply answered, 'This,' and did what lay in his path to do at the moment, trusting himself completely into the hands of his Father. This is how he endured the cross."[6]

Following the formula—For nine months of waiting, praying, and fasting—for the war, my daughter's health, my health, our finances, and a painful relationship—I tried to follow Jesus' example, the principles of Matthew 6:34, and the model of Elisabeth Elliot. For nine months, I endeavored to take one day at a time. Nine months is 270 days of living one day at a time, 270 days of not worrying about tomorrow, 270 days of handling the trouble of each day as it came, 270 days of not allowing myself to look ahead or anticipate the worries of 269 tomorrows.

Dear one, for 270 days I had to follow the formula, the five guidelines for winning over worry (see chapters 7 and 8). I had to prepare, plan, and pray. And I had to proceed. I had to live each day as it came. I had to forego my selfish desires to withdraw and give up. And, praise God, as I proceeded ahead, His ever-so-adequate provision and mercy were indeed new every morning!

Managing Affliction

Like emotional stress, physical suffering calls us to follow the principles of Matthew 6:34 and focus on one day at a time. I know people who suffer from incurable diseases, who deal with physical limitations every waking moment, who have nursed loved ones who were dying from cancer, who have children confined to wheelchairs, and who are themselves dying from breast cancer and brain tumors. How do they live when physical suffering is part of their daily reality?

Edith Schaeffer, the wife of theologian and writer Dr. Francis Schaeffer and cofounder with him of the Swiss retreat L'Abri, knows about living with a loved one's physical suffering. When medical tests revealed that Dr. Schaeffer had cancer, he told his wife those "awful words that turned our world upside down."[7]

One thing Edith did after her world was turned upside down was find a biblical perspective on the circumstances she faced. She needed "basic truth and God's Word [to] take the center of thoughts and feelings." She wrote,

> We are always living on the edge of disaster, change, shock, or attack. Peace, and the affluence to enjoy that peace, are always a false separation from the reality of the raging battle....Not only is our understanding blurred of what the Fall actually consists of, but our understanding of the absolute *marvel* of what God has done for us in making victory certain and complete is dimmed![8]

Mrs. Schaeffer knew Scripture's teaching that we will suffer in this world, and she recognized that peace and good times are fleeting on this earth. She also saw confirmed in the Bible the sterility of a life without suffering as well as God's provision for certain victory in suffering.

Preparing— So, armed with spiritual truth, Edith Schaeffer prepared for their time of physical trial. She remembers,

> I felt [it] imperative...to make a home for Fran as soon as possible, if he were to stay [in the United States] for treatment—whether he had six weeks or six months to live!...Why a "home"? I would answer that home is important to a person to help him or her get well, as well as being important for family times together if someone is dying. In either case, beauty and familiar surroundings

have an effect on the physical, psychological, and even spiritual state.[9]

Planning—Edith Schaeffer also planned. The diagnosis of cancer gave the family some waiting time, and Mrs. Schaeffer learned that "'marking time' is never the way to wait....Creative ideas need to begin to take place in one's imagination....Even in times of shock, waiting can be something more than sitting in abject fear."[10] Planning was one of the ways Mrs. Schaeffer used her waiting time. She explained, "Doing interior decorating inside your head while in a hospital or clinic waiting room is a positive creative activity—as well as a way of planning for demonstrating your love and concern for the person you love."[11]

Praying—During this waiting time, Mrs. Schaeffer also prayed. Every single day, throughout each stage of the cancer, and before, during, and after every doctor's report, Edith Schaeffer prayed. And what did she pray? "Don't let any one of us stop trusting you now, Lord. Please may our love be real for you—solid oak, not a thin veneer. This is the time that counts for your glory; don't let us blow it....Please, Father, give us victory...."[12] She also asked God to give her husband "time and strength to show forth God's strength and power to the next generation."[13]

Proceeding—Having prepared, planned, and prayed, Mrs. Schaeffer proceeded. With three days of cleaning, painting, and assembling an odd assortment of furnishings, she made a home for her beloved husband. She provided opportunities for the family to be together. She thoroughly researched cancer, chemotherapy, vitamins, and diet, and proceeded with the daily challenges of caring for a cancer patient. Mrs. Schaeffer writes, "'One-day-at-a-time' became an important measure to be constantly met....When you are supposed to die in a short period of time, the dates are more appreciated; the 'and thens' take on a bit of sparkle!"[14]

As Edith Schaeffer moved forward, so did Dr. Schaeffer. Despite his suffering, he continued to minister. He spoke to large gatherings of doctors and local residents and answered their questions about God, life, and death. He "went on in the midst of cancer, trusting the Lord, and continuing to care about other people...[realizing] there is more to life than being 'comfortable' and 'happy'; there is growth going on...."[15]

Tasting God's provision—God provided for the Schaeffers as they proceeded. Even when Dr. Schaeffer felt so dizzy he thought he couldn't speak, Mrs. Schaeffer notes that "strength came in a sufficient quantity....Just enough energy 'was given' to carry on each time. It [wasn't] that Fran felt great. Rather he felt he could ask for the Lord's strength in measure for the needs and that it wasn't time to 'give up' when he could be a help."[16]

During the five years that her husband suffered, Edith Schaeffer focused on today. She took one day at a time and relied on God to be with her. Day-to-day and moment-to-moment, she prepared, planned, prayed, and proceeded with her duties and responsibilities and with a continual outpouring of love. And day-to-day and moment-to-moment, she experienced God's provision for her. She did not give up or quit. She dealt with her emotions when they came, and she never ceased to be a selfless woman, wife, and mother. "Looking back on it," she says, "I don't think I'd do anything differently." Even as she faced enormous emotional and physical challenges, Mrs. Schaeffer lived out of God's grace each and every day.

Loving God...Even More

Now, my friend, where does today find you? What are the circumstances of *your* life? Are your emotions stretched to the limit? Is physical affliction taxing you or a loved one? What fires are purifying your faith in God? Whatever your situation, God calls you to live one day at a time. Again, quoting Jesus, you are not to "worry about tomorrow; for tomorrow will care for itself. Each day has enough trouble of its own" (Matthew 6:34).

Whether your particular challenge is physical, emotional, mental, a combination, or all-of-the-above(!), the strategy of preparing, planning, praying, and proceeding will help you draw close to God, love Him even more, manage life's demands, and win over worry—one day at a time. Then, as you proceed through each day, you will experience God's love in very personal ways as you discover His complete provision. You will witness daily miracles as you find God meeting you in the circumstances of your life and giving you the strength you need...exactly when you need it.

God does indeed enable us to live according to His instruction to focus on today. With Him, you and I can successfully climb the mountain of today, leaving the mountain range of tomorrows to tomorrow. And the peace that comes with knowing that we are following God's guidance day by day, moment by moment, frees us to better love God with all our mind.

Pressing for the Prize

❧❧❧

Brethren, I do not count myself
to have apprehended; but one thing I do,
forgetting those things which are behind and
reaching for those things which are ahead,
I press toward the goal for the prize
of the upward call of God in Christ Jesus.

PHILIPPIANS 3:13-14

$\mathcal{R}$EMEMBERING TO FORGET

∽∾

Forgetting those things which are behind...

PHILIPPIANS 3:13

$\mathcal{A}$LTHOUGH I'VE NEVER ATTENDED one of my high school reunions, I've heard about them! My friends have told me about classmates who still look the way they always did and about others whose personalities haven't changed at all. They also report that others are larger— and/or balder!—and almost unrecognizable. Also, and sadly, some who enjoyed success during their high school years have gone the way of alcoholism, suffered disabilities, and encountered other tragedies.

The past. It makes us who we are. It teaches us lessons about God, about life, and about ourselves. We learn volumes from what lies behind. But our learning must not stop there. We must then take those lessons and move ahead. And this is exactly the truth the apostle Paul teaches in Philippians 3:13-14, another one of my breakthrough passages that I want to share with you now.

After exalting Jesus Christ and exhorting us to be like Him, Paul tells us how to pursue Christlikeness. Acknowledging that he has not yet arrived in his own pursuit, Paul shares in Philippians 3:13-14 three actions that help him continue his progress toward spiritual maturity. And, my dear friend, these same truths apply to your growth, too. Paul writes,

> *Forgetting* those things which are behind and
> *reaching* forward to those things which are ahead, I
> *press* toward the goal for the prize of the upward call of
>   God in Christ Jesus.

Forgetting the Past

The first step toward living a life that pleases Christ—a life that culminates in eternal glory with our Lord—is forgetting what lies behind. The past, as you well know, isn't always easy to forget. Whether it's some previous success that has never been repeated or some failure we haven't let go of, the past can take hold of our minds and our hearts. I know, because thinking too much about past injuries, insults, and sorrows once made sadness and weeping a part of my every day.

As I shared in the first chapter, dwelling on the past— on the kind of disappointments, struggles, and failures we all experience—made me tired and depressed. My backward thoughts became a breeding ground for bitterness. The more I thought about what had happened to me— things like remembering a rejection from a boyfriend, recalling a cruel remark, being passed over after a job

interview, or reliving the days and events reflecting on
leading up to the death of Jim's father—the deeper I sank
into darkness and despair. And none of my backward
thinking produced any hope, any answers, or any solutions!

The apostle Paul's words in Philippians 3:13-14, however, came to my rescue. They gave me the guidance I
needed for overcoming—by God's grace—the daily negative lifestyle that grew out of my unhealthy dwelling on the
past. And like Paul is to me, he can be your teacher and
example of forgetting, reaching forward, and pressing on.

Forgetting completely—As we begin looking at Paul's
experience with forgetting the past, let me again say that
the past is important. It shapes us, it teaches us, and it
reminds us of God's faithfulness. Our spiritual growth,
however, can be blocked by paying too much attention to
the past. How is that?

Dwelling on the past can cause a slackening of pace in
our Christian walk. It's easy to look backward and never
move forward. As one commentator puts it, "Looking back
is sure to end in going back."[1] Christian growth—the
process of moving forward—requires looking to the future
rather than to the past. In fact, one scholar writes, "The
Christian's onward progress is hindered should he dwell on
the past full of failures and sins, full of heartaches and dis-
couragements, full of disappointments and thwarted hopes
and plans. As long as a Christian has made things right with
God and man, he should completely forget the past."[2]

Paul's language in Philippians 3 is strong! Another biblical scholar writes, "When Paul says that he forgets what lies
behind, he refers to a type of forgetting which is no mere,
passive oblivion. It is active obliteration, so that when any
thought of...the past would occur to Paul, he immediately

banished it from his mind....It is a constant, deliberate dis-
carding of any thought of [the] past...."[3] Still another schol-
arly source explains, "Forgetting is stronger in the Greek,
[meaning] 'completely forgetting'" and he translates Paul's
words, "I in fact am forgetting completely the things that
are behind."[4]

Taking Paul's advice—Christians of old took Paul's
advice to forget what lies behind much more seriously than
we do today. F. B. Meyer, writing in his celebrated devotional commentary at the turn of the century, addressed
"the Duty of Forgetting," and called for "no morbid
dwelling on the Sinful Past." Meyer appealed to his readers
to "learn to forget...and do not dwell upon past sin." He
explained, "There may be things in our past of which we
are ashamed, which might haunt us, which might cut the
sinews of our strength. But if we have handed them over
to God in confession and faith, He has put them away and
forgotten them." His advice? "Forget them, and...the sin
which has...blackened your record, [and] reach forward to
realise the beauty of Jesus."[5]

Moving forward in faith—Forgetting what lies behind is
not always easy. And note this—the word "forgetting" is in
the *present* tense. You see, forgetting is not an act done
once and for all. Instead, like Paul, we must *keep on forgetting* those things in the past that hold us back. Paul
didn't want to rest on his past accomplishments, and neither
should we. And Paul didn't want his past mistakes to keep
him from moving on, and neither should we.

So, again and again, I have told myself, "No, Elizabeth,
that is past. That is over. That is no longer real. So don't
dwell on it! Don't let it hold you back. Forget whatever

would keep you from moving forward in faith and in your spiritual growth." As I shared in a previous chapter, I've learned to look to the past only (well, most of the time!) to remember God's role in the problems and pain of yesterday—to recall His gracious provision for me, His presence, His faithfulness, and His compassion.

Looking to the past for lessons God has taught us and forgetting those elements of the past that would stymie our forward progress may sound like a tricky balance to maintain. What more does the apostle Paul teach us about "the art of forgetting" those elements of the past that would block our Christian growth and our progress toward Christlikeness?

Forgetting the Bad

One thing that moves us forward toward healthy spiritual growth is remembering to forget the bad we did before we became Christians. Before he came to know Jesus as Lord and Savior, Paul was Saul, the persecutor of Christians. He was dubbed by one scholar as "the guiding spirit of evil."[6] Paul is described as acting with "brutal cruelty…[as] a wild animal savaging a body."[7] The Bible reports Paul "made havoc of [ravaged] the church, entering every house, and dragging off men and women, committing them to prison" (Acts 8:3).

It's also quite possible that, rather than merely witnessing the stoning of Stephen, Paul was involved in the sentencing and gave his wholehearted approval to the murder (Acts 7:58; 8:1). Then, praise God, on his way to Damascus, with letters in hand from the high priest authorizing him to bind and bring Christian men and women to Jerusalem for trial (Acts 9:1-3), Paul met Jesus Christ! Only his encounter with Christ kept Paul's hands from being bloodied even further.

You and I may not have committed murder, but we probably did things before we knew Christ that we must forget if we are to grow as Christians. What can you and I do when those past sins come to mind?

First, remember, no fishing allowed!—We need to remind ourselves of the truth of 2 Corinthians 5:17—"If anyone is in Christ, he is a new creation; old things have passed away; behold, all things have become new." If you are a Christian, you—yes, you!—are a new creature. You have been created all over again. What does this mean? It means that old things, including the sin you committed before coming to know Jesus, have passed away and are gone forever! All that you were and all that you did as a non-Christian are gone forever, removed "as far as the east is from the west" (Psalm 103:12). As writer and evangelist Corrie ten Boom loved to say, "When we confess our sins, God casts them into the deepest ocean, gone forever. And even though I cannot find a Scripture for it, I believe God then places a sign out there that says, 'No Fishing Allowed.' "[8]

Dear reader, God's love for you accomplished the forgiveness of your sin, your cleansing, your new birth, and your fresh start. Sure, consequences of your actions may remain, but the sin itself is forgiven! You are covered and cleansed by Christ's precious blood. You can, therefore, go on with your life...without shame and without being held back. And you can show your love for God by refusing to dwell on what He has removed and taken care of. When your past sin comes to mind—and it will—stop fishing!

Acknowledge God's forgiveness, thank Him profusely, and move on.

Second, remember to press on!—Besides letting go of those sins committed before naming Jesus as Lord and Savior, you and I need to let go of the sins we have committed and the bad things that have happened to us since we became Christians. The apostle Paul, for instance, suffered great things for the sake of Christ (Acts 9:16). He experienced beatings, betrayal, hunger, and thirst because of his faith in Jesus Christ (see 2 Corinthians 11:23-27). God also allowed Satan to afflict Paul with "a thorn in the flesh" (2 Corinthians 12:7). Dwelling on these things and asking why they happened would have blocked Paul's spiritual growth and forward movement. Therefore, he needed to forget them...and move on.

Undoubtedly, certain events in life also need to be forgotten if we are to move on and grow in the Lord. These can be acts done to us or by us, acts that have consequences we are forced to deal with as innocent victims, acts we have witnessed. They can be acts like my daughter Katherine witnessed. As a working college student, she saw a tiny boy being physically abused by his father. Thinking quickly, her employer wrote down the man's license plate number and reported him to the police. But what was my Katherine to do with her memory of the abuse? With the sounds she had heard and the anxiety she had felt?

When she told Jim and me about the incident, we agonized with her. And we prayed—for Katherine, for the boy, for the man, and for the police. We also prayed for her to begin the process of forgetting. We encouraged her, through prayer, to leave the situation in God's capable hands and then, again through prayer, to obliterate any thought of what she witnessed. She had to go on.

Here's another example. My friend Laurie called me about her niece Anna. Anna had had an extremely abusive childhood, and her nightmares had begun again. Laurie and I knew Anna also needed to let go of the past and move on. As we talked about how she might help her niece, I mentioned, "And be sure she isn't watching too much news."

Laurie shrieked, "That's it, Elizabeth! When I was at her home, we watched the news together, and now I remember what was on the news that day. No wonder the nightmares started up again!" A news story had brought back the past for Anna when she was trying to move on from it.

Loving God...Even More

My dear friend, God wants Katherine, Anna, and you and me to move on from the suffering of the past. He doesn't want the circumstances and situations of life to weigh us down with guilt, result in bitterness, or cause us to question Him and His goodness. No, such incidents call us to love Him even more!

Whatever suffering you've experienced (from unexplainable losses to someone's thoughtless comment) and whenever it happened (whether 20 years or 2 minutes ago), God's remedy is the same. Don't bog down. Don't let it hinder your love for the Lord. No, follow the counsel of the Lord through Paul instead—Press on! Forget what lies behind. Let it lie behind you. Keep it in the past. Don't let the pain or the questions keep you down.

My dear reading friend, turn your hurting heart upward. Acknowledge that God's ways are not our ways (Isaiah 55:8), that innocents suffer when people sin, that we live in a fallen world. And then press on! Go on with life. In other words, remember to forget!

12

$\mathscr{F}$INDING THE GOLD

∾⟪⟫∾

Forgetting the past...
PHILIPPIANS 3:13 NLT

$\mathscr{F}$OR 20-PLUS YEARS, I'VE BEEN learning to apply the truths of God's Word to help me think on what is true and real and to win over worry. And now, as we're considering God's command to be "forgetting those things which are behind" and using our energies instead for pressing for the prize of God's heavenly calling, I want to pass on something that's been most helpful. I don't know where I heard it, but it really stuck with me...and by me. As the saying goes...

> *Learn* from the past,
> *log* the lessons from the past, but
> *leave* the past!

I'm sure you agree that dwelling on the unchangeable past (which is no longer true or real) can sap you of energy and deprive you of much joy. Said more positively, knowing that God is the God of our past, and entrusting it to Him, can free us to enjoy life in the present. It can also free up our energy—spiritual, mental, emotional, and physical—to focus forward on the race at hand and on "the upward call of God in Christ Jesus."

Forgetting the Good

Although it may surprise you, in order to effectively serve the Lord, the apostle Paul needed to leave behind *the good* as well as the bad of his past.

Paul forgot the good—Paul was indeed a bright and shining star! Before he became a Christian, he enjoyed a multitude of privileges as a Roman citizen and as a student of Gamaliel, the great teacher of the law (Acts 22:3). Paul's impeccable Jewish pedigree also meant he enjoyed an enviable position in society (Philippians 3:5-6).

Paul, however, chose to forget his status and the privileges of his position, regarding them as a hindrance to running the race for Christ. In answer to God's call on his life, Paul valued serving God and His eternal truth far more than the fleeting status and privilege the world offered him.

Seven missionaries forgot the good—In more recent times, C.T. Studd, like Paul, forgot the good he had enjoyed before becoming a Christian. Extremely wealthy and Cambridge educated, Studd was one of seven men from that college who ignited the great student missions movement in the nineteenth century.

As this group of men, "The Cambridge Seven," left for China, a news correspondent described them as

> standing side by side renouncing the careers in which they had already gained no small distinction, putting aside the splendid prizes of earthly ambition, taking leave of the social circles in which they shone with no mean brilliance, and plunging into that warfare whose splendours are seen only by faith, and whose rewards seem so shadowy to the unopened vision of ordinary men.

Later, before leaving on his second trip to China, C.T. Studd "invested in the Bank of Heaven by giving away all of his inheritance" except for 3,400 British pounds, which he presented to his bride before their wedding. She, too, knew about "forgetting those things which are behind." She asked, "Now, Charlie, what did the Lord tell the rich young man to do?" When C.T. answered, "Sell all," she said, "Well, then, we will start clear with the Lord at our wedding." She then gave the 3,400 pounds to General Booth of the Salvation Army.[1]

We must not forget the good—Even God's blessings can keep us from serving the Lord with all of our energy, all of our heart, and all of our self…if we hold on to them, dwell on them, and fail to press on toward spiritual growth and usefulness. The apostle Paul, six missionaries, and Mr. and Mrs. C.T. Studd moved on from the good the world offered to serve the better that God had for them…and so must we.

Forgetting Success

Paul also had to move on from the good that he experienced *after* becoming a follower of Jesus Christ. A brilliant orator, Paul led great numbers of people to salvation. He worked many miracles and healings, and Christ spoke to him three times. Paul saw visions, received revelations, was "caught up to the third heaven...into Paradise and heard inexpressible words" (2 Corinthians 12:2,4). God used Paul mightily to minister to early believers, and today his writings comprise 13 books of the New Testament.

Even ministry accomplishments, when dwelled on too long, can keep us from reaching forward in our journey toward Christlikeness. We cannot make progress when we are resting on our laurels, resting on past successes. Therefore, we must forget the good.

Forget "who you was"—I saw this truth sadly illustrated in a couple who arrived at our church fresh from serving in a fine Christian organization for ten years. They seemed to have been everywhere and done everything for Christ. As a new Christian, I saw what they had and I wanted it...for a while. But during the next decade, I saw them float along on the merits of their former service. They regularly reminded others of their ten-year term with that worthy organization...while doing nothing in the present. Drawing on their past, this couple reminded me of the joke about a man at a Hollywood party who, feeling snubbed, went from guest to guest saying, "But you don't know who I was!"

It's far too easy for us to say, like the man at the party, "But you don't know who I was...back on the East Coast, or in my old church, or where I grew up, or when I was on the mission field, or when I served with this organization. You don't know who I was!" As Dr. John MacArthur explained in a sermon, we are like the star in the sky that died, but we could see it for 30 more years. "Its brilliance," he said, "was from the past, but it was dead in the present."

God doesn't want His people to be like that star! So through Paul, He urges us to "forget 'who you was'! What are you doing now?"

Forget the good ol' days—God wants us to forget our achievements, our accomplishments, and our brilliance so that we will keep achieving and accomplishing for Him in the present. Stopping to remember the good ol' days can too easily lead to dwelling on them and neglecting our ongoing work for the Lord. Good things in the past can keep us from looking and moving and "reaching forward." Paul says, "Forget what lies behind." Whether they happened 20 years ago or yesterday, the wonderful things you have accomplished or experienced are to be forgotten. These things are dead in the present—although we don't always realize that fact.

Pastor Chuck Swindoll wrote this about some time he spent with a group of Christian leaders:"While everyone else much preferred to be on a first-name basis (rather than Reverend or Mister) one man demanded: 'Call *me* doctor.'" Chuck's advice to "Dr. Hotshot" was "get a good education—but get over it. Dig in and pay the price for solid, challenging years in school, and apply your education with all your ability, but *please* spare others from the tiring reminders of how honored they should feel in your presence. Reach the maximum of your potential—but *don't talk about it.*" He then dared his fellow pastors to remove all the diplomas from the walls in their offices and any object that promoted them and their achievements.[2] Such signs of past achievement, back in the good ol' days, mean nothing next to what we are doing for God today.

Don't forget what is yet to be accomplished—Writing about Paul's example and instruction regarding the value of forgetting the past, one scholar comments that "the memory of past successes and attainments may detain us from more splendid triumphs....[Paul did] not please himself by dwelling on...what he had accomplished. No; his thought was what was yet to be accomplished. What was there yet possible to him of Christian experience, of Christian usefulness?"[3] Paul refused to succumb to self-satisfaction. With his gaze focused on the future, Paul knew that "the Christian must forget all that he has done and remember only what he still has to do."[4]

Beloved, thank God for the good of the past, for His blessings, and for the good He has enabled you to do for Him. And thank Him for the good ol' days! But be sure to move on and serve Him in the present.

Three Steps for Forgetting

Forgetting the past is not easy to do. It's not easy to hold lightly the good God has blessed us with and used us to accomplish. And it's not easy to obey God by and not questioning the unexplainable bad that has come our way. The following three steps, however, will help you let go of the past so that you are free to press on and serve Him in the present.

Step 1: Discover the gold—Whatever has happened to you in the past and whatever is happening in your life now, look for the "gold." Look for the hidden blessing, the lesson to be learned, or the character trait being forged. Trust that because God has allowed these experiences, somewhere in them there is gold for you! And while you are looking, remember that gold isn't always easily seen or readily accessible.

How can you discover the gold? During the Gold Rush, miners dipped their pans into the dirt at the bottom of a stream and drew up a plate filled with silt, gravel, and stones. Patiently and carefully they sifted through the dirt and hoped to find gold shining purely and brilliantly through the refuse they dredged from the riverbed. Many did indeed make their fortunes...but not without a lot of work! And it may take some work on your part to find the good God is working in the bad of your life.

Without dwelling on them, take some time to think back on the "bad things" of your life. (We'll learn more about these "bad things" in a later chapter.) Look for some positive despite the negative. Look for where our merciful and loving God is working redemption in the situations. The good you find may be a lesson learned, deeper knowledge of God, or greater understanding for further service to Him and His people (2 Corinthians 1:4). Find the good—the gold—and let go of the rest! Take it with you and move on!

Step 2: Find forgiveness—Once you discover the gold, you will need to find forgiveness for the bad that resulted from your sin. As we saw in chapter 1, "If we confess our sins, [God] is faithful and just to forgive us our sins and to cleanse us from all unrighteousness" (1 John 1:9). In this truth you find forgiveness. The truth is that you *are* forgiven, and this truth cost Christ His life. Your role is to believe that you are forgiven. Let the truth of God's gracious forgiveness help you let go of the past. After all, as my former pastor asked, "Why should you remember what God has forgotten?" Just *know* that you are forgiven!

Step 3: Forgive others—Finally, having discovered the gold and found God's forgiveness, forgive those who have hurt you. Jesus modeled such forgiveness for us as, hanging on the cross, He prayed, "Father, forgive them, for they do not know what they do" (Luke 23:34). When we fail to forgive others and fail to follow Christ's example, we sentence ourselves to a life of bitterness. We also stop growing in faith, and we compromise our service and witness for Jesus. However, when we—by God's grace— extend forgiveness to those who have hurt us, we can be used mightily by God. For instance...

—Helen Roseveare, a missionary doctor who was brutally raped while serving in the Congo, forgave those who wronged her and returned to the same location for 20 more years of missionary service.[5]

—When Elisabeth Elliot forgave the men who savagely killed her missionary husband, she was able to return and continue her ministry of the gospel of forgiveness.[6]

—Evangelist Corrie ten Boom struggled greatly but found the strength to forgive the German soldier who had been the cruelest to her sister and herself while they were prisoners at Ravensbruck during World War II.[7]

Dr. Helen Roseveare, Elisabeth Elliot, and Corrie ten Boom all found freedom from the past and the freedom to press on and serve when they extended forgiveness to those who had hurt them deeply...and you and I must do the same!

Loving God...Even More

Remembering to forget the past is a shiny key to unlocking the door of days gone by and finding the gold and the freedom from a past that holds back our Christian growth. "Forgetting those things which are behind" is the first stride the apostle Paul took as he ran the race, pressed for the prize, and lived his life for Jesus Christ. So what do you need to let go of from the past? Are you resting on the laurels of past achievements for the Lord? What major accomplishment may be hindering your effort to run the Christian race today? Thank God for using you as He has. Then ask Him to show you where He would have you press on for Him.

Perhaps you are being held to the past by a source of deep pain or an experience that is hard to understand. Ask God to shine His light in your darkness (Psalm 112:4). Ask Him to help you discover the gold of His perfect work in your life. Where it's appropriate, admit any wrong acts or thoughts and ask God's forgiveness. And, when needed, ask God's help in forgiving others.

With the gold gleaned from the past and God's forgiveness both extended and received, you will more fully experience God's freeing and empowering love, an experience that enables us to love Him...even more.

13

$\mathcal{G}$OING ON AND
ON AND ON

$\sim\!\!\gg\!\!\ll\!\!\sim$

Reaching forward to those things
which are ahead...

PHILIPPIANS 3:13

$\mathcal{A}$ MISSIONARY ONCE LABORED to teach his tribal people Philippians 3:13-14, where the apostle Paul writes, "Brethren, I do not count myself to have apprehended [spiritual maturity or Christlike perfection]; but one thing I do, forgetting those things which are behind and reaching forward to those things which are ahead, I press toward the goal for the prize of the upward call of God in Christ Jesus." Several days after the lesson, one of the missionary's "students" approached him and asked permission to read the poem he had written about the meaning of Paul's words:

> Go on, go on, go on, go on,
> Go on, go on, go on.

Go on, go on, go on, go on,
Go on, go on, go on!

And there were seven more identical stanzas to his poem. This man definitely got Paul's message!

To quickly review, Paul learned *Step 1,* the importance of forgetting the elements of the past (both the good and the bad), that would hold back his spiritual growth. And now he shares *Step 2* for growing and serving the Lord— "reaching forward to those things which are ahead."

Like Paul, when we choose to forget the elements of the past that can weigh us down or keep us stuck there, when we leave the good and the bad of the past in God's omnipotent and capable hands, we make a 180-degree turn! No longer do we focus on the past. Instead, we are riveted on what's ahead. Our "no" to the past—to what is behind—is also a "yes" to the present and what is at hand. And, as you'll see now on our walk through what it means to reach forward to what is ahead, this focus on the present is vital.

Where Are You Going?

What characterizes forward-moving, focused Christians? What sets them apart? For starters...

✓   They know where they are going.

✓   They have a sense of God's call on their lives, which gives them sure direction each step of the way and makes decision-making easier.

✓   They understand the purpose of their lives.

✓   They focus on God and God-given goals,
which makes it easier to say "no" to what is
trivial.

✓   They choose wisely from among their
options, which moves them toward life
goals.

This brings us back to *energy,* that great secret to success! A forward focus gives us greater energy for reaching
our goals...which, as we just noted, are God's goals. Therefore, energy is not wasted on wondering what to do or on
wandering aimlessly from option to option. Knowing
exactly what to do and what needs to be done also dictates
where our energy is spent. A God-confidence blossoms as
we gain more certainty about what to do and about God's
enabling power to serve wherever He has placed us.

Knowing *where* we are headed and *why* is the kind of
focus Paul calls us to in Philippians 3:13-14.

Where Is Your Focus?

When Paul writes about "reaching forward to those
things which are ahead," he is likening his life to a race and
picturing himself as a runner in the act of racing toward the
finish line. His body is bent forward. His eyes are fixed on
his goal. Moving along the path God has laid out for him,
he leans forward as his feet carry him toward the finish. All
of his energy—spiritual, mental, emotional, and physical—
is committed to the race he is running, "to those things
which are ahead."

This image is quite a contrast to the paintings of an
Edwardian lady featured on some note cards I saw in a
bookstore one day! With a dreamy half-smile, this woman

lounges on a pillowed window seat. With one hand, she holds the book she's reading. With the other, she strokes the cat curled up in her lap. A gentle breeze lifts the gauze curtains to reveal a splendid day outside. Her days of simple leisure hardly reflect the way Christ means for us to live our lives. Instead, like Paul, we are to run a race toward the goal of Christlike maturity and service. Besides keeping our standards high, that prize gives us reason to go on and on and on.

Like me, you may daydream about days of leisure like the greeting card suggests. (Oh, I can taste it...feel it... smell it!) But perhaps, also like me, you realize that life is a race. And like me, you are by God's grace doing your very best to run it for and with Him. If so, here's something that helps. To stay on course, I ask myself the following questions from time to time:

- Am I focusing my efforts toward the prize that awaits at the end, or am I too content watching other people's efforts?

- Am I "training" regularly and "working out" in the daily disciplines of the Christian life?

- Am I properly fueling my body with sleep, nutrition, and exercise for maximum results?

Running the race—living for Christ and growing into His image—requires focus and discipline. And yes, rest and relaxation are important as we respond to God's call on our lives. But we are not to let the desire to rest, relax, and reward ourselves interfere with our efforts for God's kingdom. Like Paul's words encourage us, a runner's focus and mentality can fuel and jet-propel our race toward Christlike perfection.

Focusing on the Present

Here's another message from Paul: A runner who looks backward will lose the race. As we saw in previous chapters, Paul chose not to allow his past failures and accomplishments to interfere with his present efforts for his Lord. He sought instead to be "reaching forward to those things which are ahead." And that same 180-degree decision to forget the past and focus on present forward movement enables you and me to grow spiritually.

To repeat, leaving the elements of the past in God's hands—elements that would hold us back and drain us of energy—is a crucial first step in the race toward Christlikeness. Forgetting the past frees us from self-condemnation and regret so that we can enjoy God's love for us and love Him in return. As one woman shared with me after she heard this lesson on forgetting what lies behind, "This verse is for anyone who has ever made a mistake. What a splendid wave of comfort washes over me to realize the freedom to not look back over my past failures."

Recognizing God's Purpose for You

Our runner's focus on the present comes when we clearly understand the purpose of our lives. I personally discovered God's purpose for me—His call on my life—in a very special way when a woman handed me a small, flat package wrapped in muted pastels. The card read, "Thank you for your class on prayer," and the package contained a leather-bound, silver-edged book that soon broadened my prayer life.

Unfortunately that tiny prayer volume is now out of print, but here's what changed my life and polished up my purpose. Four questions were posed about our identity in Christ. Puzzled, I paused long enough to scratch my head and then went on. But the questions haunted me until one day I reluctantly tackled the questions—

> Who am I?
> Where did I come from?
> Why am I here?
> Where am I going?

The beautiful little book changed my prayers and my prayer life. But, dear friend, answering these four questions changed my life! Before I answered them, I was greatly influenced by other people's ideas about what I should do with my life and what my Christian faith should look like. A "movement" follower and a "program" participant, I allowed other people to determine my purpose. But, praise God, these four questions helped me recognize the purpose of my life and gave me life goals to focus on. Today I know...

- Who I am—I am a Christian woman, wife, mother, and grandmother;

- Where I came from—I was "in [Christ] before the foundation of the world" (Ephesians 1:4);

- Why I am here—I am here to give my life in service to God, my family, and His people;

- Where I am going—by God's amazing
grace and love, I am going to heaven!

Please take a few minutes to answer these four questions for yourself. Your answers won't be identical to mine. But they will help you grasp God's great purpose for *your* life. They will give you a sense of direction as you set your goals and plan your activities.

You may be awed like I was by the realization that God has a specific purpose for you. For me, that realization has given me a better sense of mission (I am definitely more focused as a result of glimpsing God's purpose for my life), a clearer understanding of my job assignment (I am to spend myself and be spent in service to Christ and His people), and an urgency as I go about my tasks (knowing that my time on earth is limited, I am frightfully aware of time wasted and time passing). I want to use my time and energy to achieve God's purposes and, along the way, find rest and refreshment in Him. After all, it is He who ultimately makes things happen for the kingdom. I am just thankful that He has chosen to use me in the process!

Loving God...Even More

*T*he apostle Paul was certainly used by God as he responded to the God-given purpose and driving force of his life. He wrote, "I press on, that I may lay hold of that for which Christ Jesus has also laid hold of me" (Philippians 3:12). As one scholar explains, Paul—

is trying to grasp that for which he has been grasped by Christ....Paul felt that when Christ stopped him on the Damascus Road, He had a vision and a purpose for Paul; and Paul felt that all his life he was bound to press on, lest he fail Jesus and frustrate His dream....Every [believer] is grasped by Christ for some purpose; and, therefore, every [believer] should all his life press on so that he may grasp that purpose for which Christ grasped him.[1]

Do you desire to love God...even more? Then, I beg you, center your entire being in God. Look to Him and do whatever it takes to keep from getting tripped up or stalled by the past. Focus! Reach forward! And press on for that for which you have been grasped by Christ.

14

$\mathscr{F}$OCUSING FORWARD...
AND SAILING ON!

∝∝

Straining toward what is ahead...

PHILIPPIANS 3:13 NIV

$\mathscr{M}$EET JOSEPH. HE'S AN AMAZING MAN...AND an amazing model of someone who had to forget those things that were behind, forgive those who hurt him, fix his gaze upon those things which were before, and go on and on and on. Joseph teaches us valuable lessons on pursuing excellence as we reach forward to serve God...even when circumstances are difficult and painful. His story is preserved for us in Genesis 37–50.

Pursuing Excellence

Sold into slavery in Egypt by envious brothers, Joseph chose to serve God by doing the best he could wherever he was and whatever the circumstances of his life. In Egypt he chose to forget his past in Israel and "go on"...to where he became the best slave and manager of Potiphar's household...until he was unjustly imprisoned.

In prison, Joseph made the same choices, choosing to forget the luxury of Potiphar's palace and "go on"...to where he became the best prisoner in the dungeon, and later, the best manager of the prisoners. When he was finally released from prison, Joseph again decided to forget his dismal past in a dismal dungeon and "go on"...to where he soon became the best in a government position, a priviledged position that enabled him to feed his father, brothers, and their families when they arrived in Egypt in search of food from famine-struck Israel.

Joseph shows us excellence every step of the way... through the good and the bad. Mark this lesson well!

Bearing Fruit in the Land of Your Affliction

Yes, Joseph successfully moved on from the past. But there was one thing he didn't forget—the many instances of God's goodness! In gratitude and remembrance, Joseph named his first son Manasseh, meaning "one who causes to forget," saying "God has made me forget all my trouble and all my father's household" (Genesis 41:51 NASB). Later Joseph named his second son Ephraim, meaning "fruitful," declaring "God has made me fruitful in the land of my affliction" (verse 52 NASB). Moving on from the past, he was able to bear fruit in the present. Joseph bloomed where he was planted, and God blessed him greatly.

Perhaps you, like Joseph (and like me the year our family lived in nine different places while serving as missionaries), find yourself living where you don't want to be. Many times, like Joseph, we are not where we used to be and not where we want to be...and not where we're going to be! And many times, like Joseph, we find ourselves holding positions or having responsibilities we did not choose for ourselves. In times like these, we can follow Joseph's example and...

—forget the past,
—forgive those who have caused us pain,
—focus on the present time and place, and
—follow after excellence

while expecting God to work His goodness and purpose in the circumstances. By determining to be the best we can be wherever we are, you and I can also bloom where we are planted.

So, where has God "planted" you? Are you a missionary in Africa living in a mud hut or a widow roaming through a palatial-but-empty home? Are you in a rural community of 39 people or in a metropolis of millions? Wherever God puts you, He has a purpose. Whatever the situation, it is an opportunity to "go on" and bear fruit for His kingdom. However difficult the circumstances, He will enable you to accomplish something for Him as you look to Him and focus on being useful to Him and to others.

Existing...or Serving?

It's true that difficult and painful circumstances can make it difficult for us to pursue excellence as we serve God. But circumstances that are too comfortable can have the same effect. We can become people who merely *exist* rather than ones who actively *serve* God. Content with where we are, we can fail to press forward toward Christ-like maturity.

My husband told me about a woman who lived in her dream home on a lake in middle America, thoroughly enjoying the quiet setting and leisurely pace of country living. Her husband had a once-in-a-lifetime career opportunity that required that they move to Los Angeles. She, however, had no desire to relocate, especially to Los Angeles! So she stayed by her lake…and her husband passed on his golden opportunity.

Don't you wonder if perhaps this woman and wife mistakenly thinks "the prize" is to reside on waterfront property instead of attaining the spiritual maturity that comes with forgetting the past, reaching forward, and pressing ahead toward "the upward call of God in Christ Jesus" (Philippians 3:14)? Leaving her lake meant taking a risk, making a move, and growing her faith through new changes and challenges. In this woman's case, her comfort may actually cause her faith to stop growing and her pursuit of excellence to wane.

Hear Paul's message again! He warns us against resting on past achievements or present comfort. He urges us to purposefully look ahead and to wholeheartedly reach forward. He exhorts us to continue to press on in the race to our very last breath, and to discover a deeper faith in God. For growth to occur, there must be tension in our lives. That healthy, productive tension comes from change. But it can also come from the goals we set that push us to reach and press forward in growth and from our decision to be the best we can be for Him—wherever we are. So set the goals that demand that you grow. And beware of getting too comfortable! Too much comfort invites us to watch the race rather than to energetically participate in it.

Whether we find ourselves in difficult circumstances (like Joseph) or enjoying a life of comfort utterly void of challenge (like "the lady by the lake"), we must resolve to focus on God's purpose for us and press for it...for the prize! We must choose to pursue God's will for us. Strengthened by Him, we must participate fully in the race He calls us to run. Whether we are experiencing pain or pleasure right now, we need Paul's mind-set—"One thing I do: forgetting what lies behind and reaching forward to what lies ahead, I press on toward the goal for the prize of the upward call of God in Christ Jesus" (Philippians 3:13-14 NASB).

Fixing Your Heart and Mind on God

By now I hope you realize the importance of being focused. Focus is essential to running a race because if a runner fails to focus, that runner fails! But focus—whether in an Olympic race or in our Christian walk—does not always come easily.

Here's a race I enter daily. Every day when I sit down to read my Bible, I suddenly—and amazingly!—think of all sorts of things I need to do...not only today, but for the rest of my life! I then have to focus and fight the urge to jump up and move the clothes from the washer to the dryer. Or I think of a person I need to call and instinctively reach for the phone. Again, I have to focus! It is indeed a battle to focus my mind and my heart on reading the Bible and praying. So I go to war.

The conversation I have with myself goes something like this: "No, I'll write that down and do it later. I'm going to read my Bible....No, I'll call her later. I'm going to read my Bible....No, I'll let my answering machine take that call. That's why I have it. I'm going to read my Bible....No, I'm not going to put the clothes in the dryer right now. I'm going to read my Bible....No, I'll write that letter later. I'll load the dishwasher later. I'll make the bed later. I'll call the repairman later. *I'm going to read my Bible!*"

I also imagine myself wearing mental blinders that make it impossible to see all the options available to me. But even more compelling is God's love for me. So I ask *Him* to help me focus on *Him.* I lift before Him my struggle and the concerns and duties that crowd in. I ask for His gracious strength as I seek to fix my heart and mind on Him and Him alone.

Asking God to clear my mind of all that interferes with our time together brings His peace. He enables me to focus on the time at hand, on what is true and real—time with Him—so that I can meet with Him and then go through the day loving Him with all of my freshly filled heart, soul, and mind. True to the promise of Isaiah 26:3—"You will keep him in perfect peace, whose mind is stayed on You" —God does indeed help us fix our hearts and minds on Him.

Keeping a Vigilant, Steady Focus

Throughout our busy days, whatever situations come our way, God will help us keep our focus on Him and on what lies in our path. I remember one morning when I received a telephone call from a woman who was upset with me: "You said this...and then you did that...and I don't think you should have...." I hear critical comments about a lot of things, but this time the attack was personal.

As I was listening to this woman, I also heard the front door open and a familiar "Yahoo!" My daughter Courtney stuck her smiling face around the corner of my office door and waved. She had stopped by to pick up a few papers from her files. Because Courtney lived on her college campus, every moment with her was a blessing.

I explained (I hope graciously) to the caller that my daughter had just stopped by and arranged to finish our talk later. As I hung up the phone, I noticed my heart was racing and my stomach was churning. I felt bewildered, confused, and hurt. I wanted to process all that had been said and deal with the situation...but here, before my very eyes, was my lovely daughter, innocently chattering away as I fixed us a snack. Courtney was here, Courtney was now, and Courtney was real. The phone call was already 30 seconds in the past...and I needed to forget it for the moment, reach forward to what was lying right in my path *now*—a few golden minutes of time with my daughter.

Was I going to let a negative phone call—that was over and done with—ruin my time with my daughter? Although she was an unplanned—and welcomed!—interruption, she was clearly my next assignment from God. Realizing that being with Courtney was God's will for me *now,* I turned my focus forward. I decided to be the best mother I could be at that moment. That meant "forgetting" the call for those few minutes and going on by focusing fully on my daughter. So I riveted my eyes on her and listened intently. I chose to savor the present, precious treasure of time with her.

With God's help, my focus changed from the phone call to my daughter. And, my dear reading friend, such changes in focus are part of the rhythm of life. As the events of our day change and as interruptions arise, our focus must also change. This enables us to put aside unpleasantness or pain so we can experience and enjoy whatever is happening in the present. After all, the demands of the present—the tasks to perform, the duties to fulfill, the responsibilities to handle, the people to minister to—comprise the course on which we run the race toward Christlikeness.

Hearing God's Voice

As you and I run the Christian race, many voices call us to abandon the effort. The world woos us away from following Christ and offers tempting rewards for choosing its way to what it deems "success." We feel pressure to be like people in the neighborhood or at the office, and we aren't always affirmed in our efforts toward excellence. The past would hold us prisoner, chained and bound to darker days and deeds. And the flesh calls us to "have some fun...take it easy...don't worry...take care of it tomorrow!" The world doesn't understand the Christian's race and the glorious prize that awaits. The world doesn't acknowledge the cause of Christ or value the commitment His cause requires.

Despite the din of these various voices, the Christian runner who is looking ahead and reaching forward has ears for only one voice. The runner clearly hears God's strong voice over the weaker but persistent voices of the world that call him to lesser pursuits and duller prizes. Through the pages of Scripture, God's strong voice urges us to "go on, go on, go on, go on" and offers us the encouragement we need as we serve Him.

What kind of encouragement? God's Word calls us to look ahead, to determine our God-given purpose, to "set [our] mind on things above" (Colossians 3:2) and on the goals He gives us, to be the best we can be for Him, to daily fix both heart and mind on God Himself, and to direct our focus forward every minute. God's Word also tells us to "go on." And God's Word reassures us that He is with us as we run the race, offering guidance and strength each step of the way.

Loving God...Even More

*D*ear friend, throughout life and throughout the race, discouraging voices will be loud and persuasive. Christopher Columbus experienced such voices on his journey across the Atlantic Ocean. Day after day he sailed without seeing land. And day after day his sailors threatened mutiny. They tried to persuade him to turn back, but Columbus refused to listen. At each day's end, he entered in the ship's log the two words, "Sailed on."

Those are the two words you, too, need to enter into the log of your journey, sometimes even minute by minute! You need to "sail on" as you look ahead and reach forward toward spiritual maturity and the goal of loving God with all your mind. As you focus on God, He will guide your steps, empower your service to Him, and work in you the characteristics of Christ. He will enable you to meet the demands of the present and, as the next chapter explains, to press on toward the prize. And you, fellow pursuer-of-the-prize, must go on, go on, go on, go on!

15

$\mathcal{K}$EEP ON
KEEPING ON

⟡

*I press toward the goal for the prize
of the upward call of God
in Christ Jesus.*

PHILIPPIANS 3:14

$\mathcal{W}$HEN MY HUSBAND WAS EMPLOYED by a pharmaceutical company, his manager was known among his sales force for a certain saying. No matter what happened, his words were always the same—"Keep on keeping on." If Jim did well or won the district sales contest, he was told, "Keep on keeping on." If Jim's sales fell or he lost an important account, he was again told, "Keep on keeping on." Whether Jim excelled or failed, neither was to slow his progress. He was to keep on keeping on.

Our Call to Press On

Well, dear reader, in Philippians 3:14, the apostle Paul encourages this same attitude in us toward the journey of life when he writes, "I press toward the goal for the prize

---

of the upward call of God in Christ Jesus." Up to this point in this section about "Pressing for the Prize," Paul has been pointing us toward a scriptural mind-set that is actively forgetting the past—learning from it but letting go of whatever would keep us from growing in our walk of faith. And now, as Paul ends this life-changing and life-directing exhortation, he instructs us to turn our face *toward* Jesus and focus fully on *Him*. As one commentator eloquently observed,

> We must look forward, not backward. Some men stand with their faces to the west, regretting the lost radiance of the setting sun. Others turn their gaze on the east, eager to catch the first streak of dawn. Surely the latter are the wiser. Our faces look forward that we may see the path we are about to tread.[1]

In our race toward becoming like Christ—and loving God with all our mind—we experience God's love more fully when we look to the dawning of each fresh new day. We must therefore answer God's call to press on and invest our energy on progress rather than focusing on the faded events of the past. We must reach forward by forgetting the past, concentrating on the present, and now, as Paul says, to push and press for the future "prize of the upward call of God in Christ Jesus."

How can we keep on keeping on? God gives us an easy formula for sustained growth: By (Step 1) *forgetting* what lies behind (in the past), we next (Step 2) assume a runner's posture of *reaching* forward (in the present), and (Step 3) begin the pursuit by *pressing* "toward the goal for the prize of the upward call of God in Christ Jesus" (which lies in the future—Philippians 3:14). Just as a marathon runner presses on to finish the race, so you and I must settle for nothing less than living every day for Jesus. We must give our utmost for His highest. *Pressing* means running "with utmost effort" and suggests "active and earnest endeavor." We are to "strain every nerve to pursue the ideal,"² remembering to draw on God's grace and strength each step of the way.

This pressing on toward the goal is a race we will run for the rest of our lives. And such effort can only be extended toward something significant. That "something significant" is the Savior who died for us. Focusing on Jesus is what enables us to give our wholehearted effort to the race of life. We can only keep on keeping on when we have our eyes on Him, our crucified and risen Lord.

A Grand Purpose

Purpose is paramount! I know I can't do anything, including getting out of bed on time(!), without having a sense of God's purpose for my life. Knowing my purpose—knowing that I am here to give my life in service to God and His people—is a driving motivator that keeps me keeping on in this race toward Christlikeness called life. And this is probably true for you, too. Therefore, it's important to develop goals under this broad aim of serving God with your life.

Here's one way to do this. When my husband conducts goal-setting seminars for men, he asks the men to write at the top of a sheet of paper, "What are my lifetime goals?" Then they are to answer that question by writing without stopping until Jim's timer rings after five minutes. Once they stop writing, they spend a few more minutes fine-tuning their answers. Finally Jim has the participants choose the three goals that are most important and rank them in order from most important to least important.

My story—I remember well the first-ever goal-setting seminar Jim led. It was for the two of us, and it occurred on a Sunday afternoon. We had spent a glorious and uplifting morning at church being taught, stretched, and challenged. Inspired by the worship and full of wishes and dreams, we knew we wanted to love Christ better and serve Him in some greater way. He had saved our souls, blessed our marriage and family, and given our lives purpose. Now what could we do to serve and follow Him more passionately and intently?

This conference-for-two was held in our home. As Jim and I sat facing each other at the dining table, we worked through these simple exercises that would change us forever. The desires of our full hearts spilled out on paper as we penned our responses. Little did we know that something as simple as the question "What are my lifetime goals?" could be the catalyst for grand goals that would energize us to serve our Savior. We were...and still are...willing and enthusiastic about pressing toward those goals that are enabling us now (and have been for 30 years) to reach forward and press on toward fulfilling the purpose of our lives—serving Jesus Christ!

What three goals did I define for myself that day? Here they are:

- To be a supportive and encouraging wife and mother

- To be a woman of God who is growing in knowledge and grace

- To teach the Bible so that women's lives are changed

Since setting these lifetime goals, I have known not only the purpose of my life, but the purpose for each day...and each minute in those days. Although I will never completely reach these goals, they challenge me daily to be the best I can be for God. These goals have kept me on track through the years—both the tough ones and the golden ones—and encouraged me to keep on keeping on.

Your story—Are you, my reading-and-reaching friend, focused on a specific-yet-grand purpose for your life? Can you, like Paul, talk about the "one thing" you do (Philippians 3:13)? It's good to think and dream about what you want to do for Christ, but it's essential to articulate specific lifetime goals that will fuel and further your efforts to fulfill your purpose of serving God. And what will most likely happen? Seeing your goals written out on paper will be sobering as you consider the privilege of working for God's kingdom and that high calling on your daily life. Those goals will also be very motivating as they remind you that you can, by the grace of God, do something eternally significant with your days on this earth.

If you haven't made your God-given purpose of serving Him personal by establishing some guiding goals for your life, please take the next hour to do so. Close the bedroom door, go to a coffee shop on your lunch hour, or clear the breakfast dishes off the kitchen table after everyone leaves. Spend 60 minutes with God, praying and thinking about His goals and purposes for your life. Answer the question, "What are my lifetime goals?" Then select from your list the three goals that are most significant to you as you consider God's causes. Rank them in order of importance.

And the blessed results? You won't be the same after this hour with your Lord. These 60 minutes spent reflecting on His purposes for you will be life-changing! I guarantee that you will discover new dimensions to your life. You'll find new energy for pursuing God's calling as you glimpse what you can be and do for Christ and in Him.

A Concerted Effort

Once you've set goals for your pursuit of serving God, you'll undoubtedly want to do your best and give your all to achieve those goals. You will want to press on and hold nothing back. God's ever-available grace empowers us to persevere and persist in untiring activity. And, praise the Lord, as we depend on God's guidance and His strength we are able to   press on. *He* Himself enables us to walk through our days sensitized to His presence and trusting in His perfect timing, to keep moving, keep serving, keep functioning, keep growing, keep giving, and keep pressing on toward our desire to serve Him.

"Wings Like Eagles"

Hear now God's promise of a "secret" source of energy and efforts: "Those who wait on the LORD shall renew their strength; they shall mount up with wings like eagles, they shall run and not be weary, they shall walk and not faint" (Isaiah 40:31). Did you catch it? As we press on, God is there to enable us to serve Him.

Oh, how I hope you have experienced days when mounting up with wings like an eagle and pressing on seem effortless and enjoyable as you soar with God! What a thrill! But perhaps you've also experienced the kind of day that prompted Amy Carmichael, pioneer missionary to India, to pray, "Father, I'm not soaring today. Help me." In her writings, Miss Carmichael pens her heavenly Father's response, "Daughter, soaring is not always flying high above the world. Sometimes one is soaring only two feet above the ground, just enough to keep you from getting tangled in the thorns and crashing against the rocks."[3]

It's true that some days you and I may feel that we're soaring awfully close to the rocks! We may feel too tired to run, and our walk may not be much more than a limp or a stagger. Yet on such days, we are to keep facing forward. (As a chief research scientist of General Motors noted, "The enthusiast fails forward"!)[4]

But even when we weaken, and even when we "fail forward," we are to rest in the Lord and rely on Him. You see, He's in control. And because of this truth, we can keep on keeping on, whatever obstacles and distractions arise. Pressing on is our duty and, as one commentator wisely points out, "We are not blamed if we have not yet reached that crown of goodness. But we are blamed if we are not pressing on to it and rest contented with anything short of it."[5]

Focusing on the Goal

Paul kept pressing on. And one reason he was able to do so was his focus on the goal. You see, the primary aim of his life was to *finish* the race. Have you yet made the decision to press forward for Christ until the end of your life? I have to admit that when I first became a Christian, I had not made that decision. I daydreamed instead of the world's ideal goal—retirement! I believed that, at a certain time, Jim and I would quit working and together live out the fantasies pictured on the travel brochures and maps I had collected.

My husband, however, had very different ideas! Jim firmly told me, "I'm never going to retire." With that statement, my daydreams vaporized, and I was sobered to recognize God's plan for His people...and for me. I realized that living for Christ means *living* for Him...all the way and to the end. We are called to live for Christ every day, not just until some magical, arbitrary age or income level when we stop serving others and serve only ourselves. No, we are called to press on and to *finish* the race.

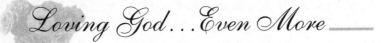

Loving God...Even More

*E*very participant in any race knows that finishing the race is not easy. And the same is true for us as we love God and run the race "for the prize of the upward call of God in Christ Jesus." Sometimes along the way we may have to follow the example of the ice skaters my family and I watched one year during the winter Olympics. We watched the skating competition—but we certainly didn't enjoy it! Instead, holding our breaths and biting our nails, we endured it. During both the women's and men's events, I kept thinking, "If anyone just stays standing, they're going to win the gold medal!" Every single skater fell. But what happened after each fall was, for me, more spectacular than the skating feats. Each skater got up and went on!

One skater even fell three times, but got right back up three times, and went on to finish.

The best ice skaters in the world were falling. Every one of them fell—but every one of them got up. During their long years of training, they had learned to always continue to the end. They had learned, among other things, to keep on keeping on. And because they did so, they were indeed winners. In fact, when the skating medals were presented at the Olympics that year, each one was awarded to a competitor who had fallen, gotten up, and finished!

Dear friend, we are to do the same. Our love for God compels us to!

16

$\mathscr{P}$RESSING TOWARD GOD'S PURPOSE

cᐰ‿ᐱ

I press toward the goal for the prize
of the upward call of God
in Christ Jesus.

PHILIPPIANS 3:14

$\mathscr{R}$ETIREMENT. IT SEEMS LIKE PEOPLE'S entire lives center around this word...and life goal! And statistics tell us people are retiring earlier and earlier. And sadly, many of them are also retiring from active Christian life and service to God's people. However, fellow runner-of-the-race, this is not in God's plan! As you turn through the pages of Scripture, you won't find one saint who quit. Although many wanted to (do you remember Elijah, Jonah, and David?), not one did. Instead they kept pressing on toward God's purpose for their lives. Consider the following roll call of saints.

People in the Bible Who Focused to the End

Abraham—Throughout his life, Abraham responded to God's commands to move. He lived in tents, and his nomadic lifestyle represented his search for "the city... whose builder and maker is God" (Hebrews 11:10). And how did Abraham's life end? He died without receiving the fulfillment of God's promises of land, a vast number of descendants, and great blessing (see Genesis 12:1-3 and Hebrews 11:39). Abraham could have quit, but he desired "a better, that is, a *heavenly* country" (Hebrews 11:16). So Abraham pressed on...until he died.

Moses—Aged and weary, Moses kept on (and on and on!) serving the Lord. At one point, he even needed the help of Aaron and Hur to hold his hands up so that God would continue to bless the Israelites' efforts in battle (Exodus 17:8-13). Yes, Moses could have quit...but he didn't. Instead, he got the help he needed to raise his hands heavenward.

Later, because Moses failed to obey God and trust Him for water at Meribah (see Numbers 20:7-13), God did not allow him to cross into the Promised Land he had waited 40 years to enter. Again, Moses could have quit serving God...but he didn't. Instead, he went on and spent the rest of his days teaching the law, preparing the priests, and encouraging Joshua to lead God's people into the land his feet would never touch.

Samuel—The priest Samuel was called by God to be His prophet. But later the people of Israel rejected his leadership and asked him to appoint a king over them so they would be like their neighboring nations (1 Samuel 8:1-5).

Most people quit after being rejected, but Samuel didn't. Instead he kept on praying and preaching (12:23), and he spent the rest of his life helping Saul, the man who took his place as the leader of the nation.

David—King David passionately yearned to build a temple to God. But the Lord Almighty said to David, "You shall not build a house for My name, because you have shed much blood on the earth in my sight" (1 Chronicles 22:8). But instead of quitting, David kept pressing on for the Lord. He spent his last days making plans and gathering materials so that his son Solomon could build the temple (1 Chronicles 22:5-19).

Paul—In prison, Paul spent his final days writing letters that would guide the church of Jesus Christ in the future. He did not allow his impending death to shift his focus away from Jesus Christ and His people. Oh no! Paul kept on pressing on to the end of his life by offering encouragement, exhortation, and comfort through his pen.

John—Exiled to the island of Patmos in his old age, the apostle John could have quit. After all, his service for Christ had seemingly earned him only disgrace and dishonor. But John kept on pressing on. In his nineties, he was blessed with "the Revelation of Jesus Christ" (Revelation 1:1). The 22 chapters of the book of Revelation tell what will take place before and when the Lord returns. John served out his purpose as prophet with words that still speak to us today.

Jesus Christ—God's Son knew about the cross, but He pressed on toward it. When it was time, He endured it to the end (Hebrews 12:2). As He hung dying on that cruel instrument of torture to save you and me from our sins, He uttered three simple words—"It is finished" (John 19:30). Jesus, our Savior and our Lord, pressed on to the end.

The list of God's people who pressed on toward God's purposes and served the Lord until the end of their lives goes on and on. At one time or another during the race, each of the men of faith just mentioned had a valid reason to quit. People told them "No!" God told them "No!" to something they wanted. Circumstances seemed to scream "No!" to their personal desires. Yet not one of them quit, resigned, or retired. They knew they hadn't finished the race, that there was more work to be done, that their purpose wasn't fulfilled, and that God had other plans for them and could still use them. They knew that by God's grace they could make a difference for His kingdom right up until the day they left this earth and went to be with Him. They pressed on.

You and I may not be called by God to achieve anything near the magnitude of these men's accomplishments. However, God does view our sphere of service and responsibility as equally important. In my case, God has called me to press on in my service as a wife, a mother, and a teacher in the body of Christ. The examples of David, Paul, and the others encourage me to reach forward daily and press on to the end. These saints had a clear vision of God's purposes for them, which inspired them in their calling (and inspires me in mine) to press on toward the end in service of the Almighty.

People in Our Time Who Focused to the End

Examples that instruct and inspire us to press on are available in our time as well as in the Bible. Two women have especially modeled for me the kind of faith and love for God that keeps us pursuing God's purposes and "the goal for the prize of the upward call of God in Christ Jesus." The first is Corrie ten Boom.

In *The Five Silent Years of Corrie ten Boom,* Corrie's assistant, Pamela Rosewell, writes about Corrie's ministry during the final five years of her life. At age 86, Corrie suffered two debilitating strokes that left her unable to speak and barely able to move. Yet, until her death at age 91, she received visitors and interceded in prayer for others. By doing so, she modeled her trust in God and love for Him to everyone in her presence. Although her ministry moved from public to private, from platform to pallet, from preaching to praying, Corrie ten Boom pressed on to the end.[1]

The other woman whose example has greatly encouraged me is Shirley Price, teacher and creator of the curriculum piece entitled *God's Plan for the Wife and Mother.*[2] She delivered her final messages on Wednesday mornings in late 1974 at First Baptist Church of Van Nuys, California. Although undergoing radiation and chemotherapy for the cancer that would take her life on January 29, 1975, Shirley pressed on and finished those eight sessions that would help countless Christian wives and mothers. I was one of those recipients who later benefitted from her tapes and materials. Focused on her goal of serving Jesus and His people, Shirley pressed on toward God's purpose.

Christians who are focused on "the prize of the upward call of God in Christ Jesus" know that the prize awaits them at the *end* of the race. Although minor rewards come along the way, the highest honor doesn't come until we've run the entire race. So, acting on our love for God, we are to press on and serve Him every day of our lives. Then we will receive the prize as we see face-to-face the Lord who Himself endured to the end.

Running Unencumbered

The writer to the Hebrews knew about running the race and pressing toward God's purposes. He exhorted us to "lay aside every weight, and the sin which so easily ensnares us," and "run with endurance the race that is set before us" (Hebrews 12:1). Running the race is definitely easier when we're not weighted down or encumbered by sin. Here are some questions to help you evaluate your present running condition.

- What habits, thought patterns, or activities are holding you back or slowing you down?

- What goals are keeping your pursuit of God from being the most important activity in your life?

- What messages from the world are drowning out God's call to you?

- What do you need to lay aside so that you can better serve God?

I asked my husband what he's had to lay aside through the years in order to run the race and serve the Lord. Jim laughed and admitted, "Always television and food!" He knows that excess in these two areas is an encumbrance for him. So take an inventory of things that keep you from giving your whole heart to the race God has called you to run. Lay aside the useless, the wasteful, the meaningless, and the unimportant that clutters your life. You'll be freer to serve God with all your being.

A Look in the Mirror

Read again Paul's words in Philippians 3:13-14: "Forgetting those things which are behind and reaching forward to those things which are ahead, I press toward the goal for the prize of the upward call of God in Christ Jesus." These are the words of a man who knows the purpose of his life and who is focused on that goal. Have you, like Paul, determined your purpose in Christ? If so, are you doing your best to serve God and achieve that goal? Are you experiencing His grace as you try? Are you keeping your eyes on Jesus and letting Him inspire you along the way? Are you committed to press on to the end of your life? And are you laying aside whatever entangles you?

We who name Christ our Lord and Savior are called to love Him with all our heart, soul, and mind. This command gives our lives purpose, richness, and a significance that enhances our walk with the Savior. May we seek nothing other than to follow Him to the end, to exhibit His radiance along the way, and to accomplish His purposes for us.

Loving God...Even More

Do you realize that you are now more than halfway through our discussion of loving God with all your mind? So, at this midway point, I want you to consider how God has been at work in your life. Instead of thinking on "if onlys" and "what ifs," are you concentrating on what is true and real—God's love, His provision, His ways—and His timing in your life? Are you addressing the concerns of today, knowing that today is all you can do anything about? Are you trusting in God and leaving your past in His hands, forgetting the good as well as the bad that would keep you from serving Him wholeheartedly? And finally, are you looking ahead, reaching forward, and pressing on toward Christ by serving Him where He has placed you?

If you can answer *yes* to one or more of these questions, please be encouraged! God is transforming you into the image of His Son! As you continue to experience God's transforming love and find yourself loving Him more in return, you will experience a deeper, richer relationship with your Lord. And that relationship is key to a fulfilling life. After all, it is God's love that keeps us focused on the eternal and spiritual aspects of all we do.

In fact, in one of my favorite *Cathy* cartoons, Cathy's mother offers her daughter some advice about focus. As Cathy and her mother shop in the mall, Cathy laments, "Behind me all I see is a trail of relationship blunders." Mother sagely replies, "Don't look back, Cathy."

Next Cathy complains, "Above me all I see are balloons, and when I look down I see that they are attached to strollers full of babies that aren't mine." Again Mother advises, "Don't look up. Don't look down."

Cathy then cries, "Ahead of me all I see is the most romantic day of the year—Valentine's Day—and no man." Mother summarizes, "Don't look back, up, down, or ahead."

With her eyes covered, Cathy says, "Now I can't see anything at all." Mother comes through again, "Trust me, life is less confusing this way."[3]

Like Cathy, we can't follow her mother's advice. We are not to go through life with blinders on. No, we are to have our eyes open and focused on Christ! You see, if we aren't focused on Him, life will indeed be confusing. It is our focus on Jesus, our relationship with Him and our commitment to serving Him...as best we can and as long as we live...that gives significance and purpose to our lives.

But, as we've noted again and again, our efforts to serve God and to live for today, forget the past, and focus fully on the present are not things we are to do on our own. This call to "love God with all your mind" is a call to experience His grace. From Him we receive a new sensitivity to His presence, a better understanding for what He has called us to do, and deeper joy in getting to know Him better as we walk with Him through the minutes of every day.

Now I ask you, how could you help but love—more and more with the dawning of each fresh new day—the One who gives your life purpose? How could you not love the One who enables you to fulfill that purpose, and who promises you the reward of life eternal with Him when you finish running the race?

Counting on God's Goodness

❧❧❧

We know that all things
work together for good
to those who love God,
to those who are called
according to His purpose.

Romans 8:28

17

$\mathscr{T}$RUSTING THE LORD

❧

We know that all things
work together for good....

ROMANS 8:28

$\mathscr{I}$T WAS THE DAY OF OUR MONTHLY committee meeting. Eager to plan future events for the women of the church, our leadership group had gathered in the Fireside Room...but something was wrong. Our chairman, who had reminded each of us about the meeting and asked us to please be on time, wasn't there. After waiting for several minutes, we decided to start the meeting without her. Later, as we neared our dismissal time, Bonnie calmly arrived. Smiling broadly, she announced that she had just experienced "another opportunity to trust the Lord."

Then Bonnie shared her "opportunity." Earlier that day, while at the public park, one of her four children had disappeared. Bonnie told us of her initial panic and near-crippling fear. However, in order to think clearly enough to deal with the situation, she had sought to focus on God instead of listening to her raging emotions. Her conversation with herself went like this: "Was God in control? Yes! Did God know where her son was? Of course! Was God able to take care of him? Definitely! Could God help her? Most certainly!"

And what happened? As Bonnie turned her turbulent thoughts to God and considered His presence, His power, His knowledge, and His involvement in her life, she was able to logically and systematically develop a plan of action for finding her son. She also followed the lessons taught in the first three Scripture passages we've looked at. Bonnie thought on what was real, not on any "what ifs" or "if onlys" (Philippians 4:8). She dealt with this assignment from God as it arrived and relied on Him to meet the challenge (Matthew 6:34). And, leaning on God, she focused on the present until the emergency was over (Philippians 3:13-14).

"Another opportunity to trust the Lord" seems to arise almost daily for many of God's children, doesn't it? As Bonnie's experience teaches us, the three passages we've already looked at can help us when such "opportunities" present themselves. And now here's another jewel from Scripture that can help you and me in any and every situation. It's Romans 8:28: "And we know that all things work together for good to those who love God, to those who are called according to His purpose."

Knowing God

When Bonnie told the leadership committee about her experience, I realized that she was able to face her frightening situation because she knew about God and His great love for her and her son. Bonnie knew God and His Word well enough to put her trust in Him. Her knowledge of God gave her hope. And that kind of knowing God determines our view of life and how we approach the challenges—our "opportunities to trust in the Lord"—each day!

As we begin the second half of this book, you'll notice a shift from the practicalities of daily life to an emphasis on God. If we are to live in close relationship with God, and if we are to serve Him and His people as He has called us to, we must, as one pastor observed, "see God as the God of the Bible—supreme, sovereign, and sensitive." He goes on to write,

> The Christian life is kept fine-tuned by biblical theology. We should always interpret experience by truth—we should always filter every pain through the lens of deity. When God is in sharp focus, then life is also undistorted.[1]

An it's true! When God is in sharp focus for us, we are a step closer to loving Him with all our mind. God also uses these biblically sound thoughts to help us respond to the events in our lives calmly, rationally, and with hope because we know Him. In fact, when we acknowledge God's supreme role in our lives and set our minds on Him, He enables us to be filled with hope.

Knowing God the Father

Have you ever met someone with bright eyes and a ready smile, whose positive outlook on life gives out a con-tagious energy? That person's secret may be knowing that God's great love for him or her means that everything that happens—in the present as well as the past and the future—will be for the good in the hands of our heavenly Father. This kind of Christian is confident that God watches over every aspect of His children's lives. Therefore, every event can be greeted with this knowledge. As a result, an enthusiasm for life is established and rooted in the knowledge of the God who gives us the promise of Romans 8:28.

As we begin now to look at this magnificent promise—and truth!—from the Bible, keep in mind a few background facts. In the book of Romans, the apostle Paul thoroughly and powerfully presents the doctrine of justification by faith. And in chapter 8, Paul affirms the blessed position of those of us who name Jesus as Lord and Savior. By virtue of His death for our sins, we are accepted by God as His children.

Paul then offers believers hope and comfort in their trials as he explains that the very trials that threaten us are actually "overruled" by God.[2] As Paul himself writes, "We know that all things work together for good to those who love God." This truth of Romans 8:28, a verse much loved by many Christians, gives us knowledge of God that bears the fruit of hope in our lives. I especially love the word "know" toward the beginning of this verse. It's a little word that means you and I have some for-real truths we can think on (Philippians 4:8)! What is it we can know?

Knowing God Is at Work

I once met with a woman to talk about some problems in her life that were not going away. As she spoke, her tale turned to her childhood and the extreme poverty and backwardness of her early home. It didn't take me long to see that this dear struggling woman was allowing these past circumstances, as difficult as they were, to affect her present situation...and was blaming God for both.

And this is common. Whenever tough times come our way, we can find ourselves falling into that same trap of thinking that God made a mistake...that He wasn't there when we needed Him. Thoughts like these rob us of our hope.

The Bible, however, describes a God who is perfect in His wisdom, His ways, and His timing. He is a God who is with us always, and a God who loves us. During our tough times, we must turn to these biblical truths about God and let them comfort and assure us of His presence. In our trials and traumas, we must believe the Bible's teaching that God was and is with us always, that He doesn't make mistakes, and that He is always in control.

Through God's inspired Word, He reminds us that He, the Divine Designer, knows what He is doing. He reveals that our history, whatever our experience, is not an error, but is, in fact, a part of His plan. And the result? Reminded that God is in control, we can then face life with hope in Him. And there's more good news! With this truth in mind, we don't need to use up our time and energy trying to reconcile some of the harsher aspects of reality (cancer, airplane crashes, incest, victims of drunk drivers). We can instead—by faith—and by His grace—acknowledge that His ways are not our ways (Isaiah 55:8-9).

So what could the woman I was counseling with do—and what can you and I do—to be more sensitive to God's presence?

Step 1: List the negatives in your life—By negatives I mean the things you don't like about yourself or about your life situation. Your list may include your background, your parents (or lack of them), your siblings, your appearance, your abilities, your personality, your marital status, your children (or lack of them), your finances, and whatever challenges you may currently face.

Step 2: Acknowledge God in the "negatives"—God knew, God allowed, and God permitted. And, as Romans 8:28 states, God overrules and causes all things—including what you perceive to be "negatives"—to work together for your good.

Step 3: Thank God for each "negative"—More specifically, thank Him for His promise to work for your good and for your spiritual growth in everything in your life, even in what you don't like. Remember that God has designed your life (Psalm 139:13-16). He has a plan for your life (2 Timothy 1:9). And He is actively working out His will through the people, events, and circumstances of your life—past, present, and future, positive and negative.

Dear friend, there has never been a mistake, and there never has been or ever will be even a split second when God is not present with you, superintending and being actively involved in your life. Acknowledging that God has planned your life can help free you from bitterness and resentment toward people, events, and circumstances. It also gives you hope! You become a hope-filled Christian when you remember—and grow to know—that God is the author of every moment of your life.

Knowing God Works All Things Together

And what about the unexpected events? The seemingly coincidental things that happen to you? Those "chance" moments you are an innocent victim? And the times when you are guilty of sin? Because God is God, He is able to weave together every single aspect and event in your life and produce something good of it. Because God is God, He also causes everything in your life "to cooperate to the furtherance and final completion of His high design."[3] Furthermore, because God is God, He is able to overrule all of the evil in your life and cause it to work together for good. Hope comes to our hearts when we know—and remember —that God "works together" all things—the bad, the good...and the mysterious!

You'll love the chapter that follows! It gives us even more glorious assurance about the puzzling details of our lives. We'll grasp even more about this triumphant truth of Romans 8:28—a truth that highlights God's love for us and His awesome almighty power at work in our behalf. But first I want us to consider how to further pursue...

Loving God...Even More

Think about the marvelous truth of Romans 8:28 for a minute. That's what I was doing one day while I was in the kitchen mixing up a chocolate cake...and meditating on this hope-inducing scripture. As I assembled the items needed to make a family favorite, I couldn't help but compare the basic recipe for the chocolate cake I was making to the makeup of common, everyday life:

—Begin with bitter chocolate.
—Stir in some dry, tasteless flour.

—Add several raw eggs and some sour milk.
—Mix these and several more ingredients
  thoroughly.
—Bake the batter in a hot oven.
—The end result: a lovely chocolate cake.

Now think about your life—the bitter, the dry, the raw, the sour, the mixing, and the heat. Sounds bad, doesn't it? And it feels bad when it's happening! But in God's hands, these things—these unpleasant and uncomfortable and un-lovely elements and components of life—will result in something good. That's the promise and the hope of Romans 8:28! In God's hands, the ingredients of our lives will always work out ultimately for our good and, even better, for His eternal purposes.

The next time you are facing the bitterness, the sour-ness, the agitation, or the heat of life, let this promise encourage you to trust in the Lord and to love Him with all your mind. "Know" that God is in control...and that His end will be "good." "Know" that He will "work together" "all things" for "good." As the saying goes, "If you are taking a beating, cheer up! God is just stirring the batter to bring you a blessing!"

18

$\mathcal{K}$NOWING
GOD'S PROMISE

❦

We know that all things
work together for good....

$\mathcal{H}$OW COULD WE SUM UP the previous chapter and what we've been learning about God from His promise in Romans 8:28? Seven words seem to say it all: "God is in control of all things." That, dear reader, is the truth of Romans 8:28. And there is no fine print to this promise. There are also no disclaimers. All things and every thing—every event, every person, all of the past, all of the present, all of the future—falls under God's jurisdiction.

Knowing God Uses All Things

Are you still wondering, "*All* things"? Well, look one more time at this truth at the top of this page. That's exactly what this God-inspired, God-breathed scripture states. So now we ask, What kinds of "all things" does God work for our good?

All things includes the most pressing problem you currently face—Fill in this blank: "My Number One problem is _____."

Each day I identify the greatest challenge I face and then reaffirm that God has promised to work that very thing for good in my life. My outlook on that problem suddenly changes when I recall God's promise to turn something very bad—the worst thing in my life!—into something good. Reviewing Romans 8:28 points me to God and encourages me to count on His goodness. It gives me dazzling hope for the day ahead, a day that includes my Number One problem.

All things includes good things—Ministry opportunities, a promotion at work, a move to a different city, graduation from college, and a new job are some of the good things that God can use to spark new growth in us. Each of these good things—and any others you might add—carries with it a degree of challenge as you attempt something you've never done before. So, whenever you begin to feel flustered or frustrated by new and challenging circumstances, remember to count on your good, powerful God and His promise to you. He causes the good things in your life to work for good as you learn new skills and grow to greater levels of faithfulness, wisdom, and trust.

For instance, one good thing God uses in the lives of His married couples to cause growth is a baby, a fact I recalled one day as I was making phone calls to invite our church staff wives to a spring luncheon. One of our women had just brought her first baby home from the hospital. As I was dialing Dina's number, I thought back to Jim's and my first days of parenthood—and put the phone down. I decided to give Dina a few more days to adjust to being a mom.

A baby is indeed a miracle, a precious gift from God, and a *very* good thing (Psalm 127:3-5). But every mother will tell you that a baby causes a woman to stretch and grow! For instance, being a parent truly is an assignment from God that He uses to make parents more Christlike through countless opportunities to die to self and dive into nonstop care-giving!

All things includes bad things—The world is full of tragedy, pain, evil, suffering, and heartache. But Romans 8:28 teaches us that God uses even these bad things for our good. That means there can be no completely bad things. What a comfort and hope this is when we face the inexplicable occurrences and tragedies of life!

And unexplainable occurrences and tragedies happen! I know this personally. And I also know it because others have come to me burdened by the death of a child, unemployment, abuse, estranged family members, divorce, a handicapped child, and cancer. And what about an angry phone caller, a friend's snub, a misunderstanding, a canceled vacation? In these instances—and more!—we must remember God's promise!

Hear this explanation regarding Romans 8:28 and such bad things: "Paul is not saying that God prevents His children from experiencing things that can harm them. He is rather attesting that the Lord takes all that He allows to happen to His beloved children, even the worst things, and turns those things ultimately into blessings."[1]

What a wonderful God we have who *would* do this, and what a powerful God we have who *can* do this!

All things includes large things—I certainly heard testimony to this truth one Wednesday night at the weekly college Bible study that used to meet in our home. My husband had helped the young man who was to teach that night on Romans 8:28. When this collegian got up and announced his topic, we saw many stifled yawns of boredom as he read the familiar text out of his Bible. Quickly, however, all of us were drawn into Paul's message as this college student told about the large and bad thing that had happened to him.

We were speechless as our "teacher" described the car accident he had been in, his stay in the hospital, the amputation of his leg, his recovery process, his physical therapy, and the finding and fitting of an artificial leg. He shared openly about his struggles—emotional, physical, and practical—to adjust to a new way of life. The path to an athletic scholarship was closed to him forever, and his plans for the future were undone by that tragic accident. As our friend explained how he had relied on the powerful truth and promise from God in Romans 8:28, that verse was brought to life for us.

How had God used a car accident and the loss of a leg for good in this gentleman's life? First, the young man explained, the hospital stay gave him time to take a spiritual inventory and make fresh commitments to God. During that time on his back, he also listed the many reasons he still had for giving thanks to God. He also shared that relationships with his family were strengthened as they gathered around him during the crisis. And with the death of his athletic dreams, he had made a choice to concentrate on ministry.

Because of the large, bad thing that happened to him, our friend was attending a Christian college, participating as a student body officer majoring in Bible, leading a college Bible study, and aiming for seminary in preparation for a life of ministry to the God who saved not only his soul, but his life.

All things includes small things—While the bad in our lives may not be on the scale of this younger friend's experience, all of us have had experiences that we label "bad." And, like the small irritation that causes a pearl to grow, even relatively small "bad things" can cause the pearl of greater faith to take shape in our lives as we see God act according to the promise of Romans 8:28. For me, even a small thing like an insult turns me to Romans 8:28 for hope.

One Sunday morning I was starting up the stairs at church. I had gotten up early to read my Bible, pray, and study the lesson I was going to teach in the women's Sunday school class. As I headed toward the classroom, a woman stopped to talk to me...and shared words that hurt me deeply.

Suddenly the benefits of my early-morning Bible study, prayer, and lesson preparation disappeared. The joy of being at church also evaporated. I felt empty and hurt. How could I teach a lesson on God's grace and goodness right now?

I decided to try to do what I've been sharing in this book. First, I had to think about what was real. This woman really had said those hurtful words, but I had to chose not to speculate beyond her words about her

motives or about any incident when I might have offended
her.

For the moment I also chose to forget the incident. I
would deal with it later. Right then, however, I had to focus
on the task at hand—on what was real. Between the stairs
and the classroom door—about a 45-second walk—I had
to shift my sights to the lesson I was to teach and the ladies
who were waiting for me. I asked the Lord to calm my
thoughts and emotions, to help me forget for the time
being, honor my earlier preparation, and to use me to
share a helpful message with the class.

And I prayed! "God, You knew from before the foundation of the world that on *this* morning...at *this* time...*this*
woman...would say *this* to me." You see, that incident was
no surprise to God! No, He knew all about it and had sovereignly permitted it! So I prayed, "Thank You for believing
that I am able to handle this. And thank You that You have
promised to work this insult for good in my life." I found
strength and hope in God's promise to work an insult for
my good and my growth.

All things includes people—In the Old Testament, the
story of Queen Esther is an intriguing example of how God
uses people in our lives. Who were the significant people
in the lovely Esther's life? Answer: Her devoted cousin
Mordecai, the helpful eunuch Hegai, her temperamental
and distant husband, King Ahasuerus, and the evil villain
Haman. And how did God work through the people in this
queen's life?

> Mordecai—An orphaned Jewish girl, Esther
> was raised by Mordecai.

King Ahasuerus—When King Ahasuerus divorced
the queen, he chose Esther to become his
new queen.

Hegai—In her difficult situation, God gave
Esther favor in Hegai's eyes, and he gave her
preferential treatment.

Haman—God then used Esther's position as
queen to deliver His people from the evil
plotting of their enemy Haman.

Through the people placed in Esther's life, God provided love, advice, position, and safety for a girl without
parents and in a hard situation, while at the same time
accomplishing His purposes in history.

Just as God used good and bad—and absent—people
for Esther's good and His purposes, He will do the same
for you. Whether an individual brings you joy or sorrow,
pleasure or pain, comfort or conflict, he or she has come
from the hand of God...and He uses every single person
for your good and His purposes.

So how do you view your parents, your spouse, your
in-laws, your children (whether toddlers or teens), your
supervisor, even the angry stranger who yells at you from
a passing car? In light of the truth of Romans 8:28, you can
view these people—indeed, all people!—as part of all that
God is using for good in your life. You can count on the
good that will come from *every* relationship, no matter how
difficult or painful it is. When it comes to the people in
your life, remember, *It's not them, it's Him!* This will free
you from resentment, bitterness, and blame.

All things includes all things—

> No matter what our situation, our suffering, our persecution, our sinful failure, our pain, our lack of faith—in those things, as well as in *all* other *things,* our heavenly Father will work to produce our ultimate victory and blessing. The corollary of that truth is that nothing can ultimately work against us. Any temporary harm we suffer will be used by God for our benefit (see 2 Corinthians 12:7-10)....*All things* includes circumstances and events that are good and beneficial in themselves as well as those that are in themselves evil and harmful.[2]

As nineteenth-century preacher and teacher D.L. Moody wrote beside Romans 8:28 in the margin of his Bible, "If our circumstances find us in God, we shall find God in all our circumstances."[3]

Knowing God's Promise

Knowing God and trusting in His promise in Romans 8:28—that He causes all things to work together for good—gives us hope. It also eliminates negative responses that block spiritual growth and interfere with daily duties. For instance,

> *Doubt*—You never need to wonder about the events in your life. Why? Because "we know *with an absolute knowledge* that for those who are loving God, all things are working together resulting in good, for those who are called ones according to His purpose."[4]

Emotion—You can respond to good or bad situations alike—with faith and feelings grounded in the knowledge that God is at work in the painful, the tragic, and the disappointing.

Bitterness—You can guard against bitterness taking root in your heart by believing the truth of the assurance of God's promise.

Negative responses—You will receive strength to persevere rather than succumb to depression, discouragement, despair, defeat, anger, wrath, and frustration.

Manipulation—You will stop trying to take matters into your own hands and trust God instead, having something of a hands-off approach to life.

Loving God...Even More

*W*hat honor we give to God when we love Him, when our thoughts about Him and His hand in our lives are true! And what hope and encouragement the truth of Romans 8:28 brings to our aching souls! God has given us a promise. He assures us that He controls all things, and He works all things for our good. This means we can look at each challenge and trial, each disappointment and tragedy life brings as another opportunity to trust the Lord.

My friend, when our hope is in the Lord, we know that everything that happens to us—our most pressing problem, the good things, the bad things, the large things, the small things, indeed *all* things—will be used by God to bless us and make us more like Jesus (verse 29). With David, we can confidently proclaim, "Surely goodness and mercy shall follow me all the days of my life" (Psalm 23:6).

$\mathscr{B}$ECOMING
FAITH ORIENTED

*We know that all things work together
for good to those who love God,
to those who are called
according to His purpose.*

ROMANS 8:28

$\mathscr{T}$HE WOMEN FROM OUR CHURCH WERE crowded into a large conference room for our annual retreat. We were meeting at the headquarters of Campus Crusade for Christ which, at that time, was in Arrowhead Springs, California. Our speaker was Ney Bailey from their staff, and I still remember the story she told that first evening—a story that I read again later in her book *Faith Is Not a Feeling....*

One quiet summer day, Ney was meeting in the Colorado Rocky Mountains with 35 other women leaders from Campus Crusade. Suddenly sirens broke the peaceful stillness and megaphones barked, "Evacuate immediately! Flashflood coming! Evacuate immediately!"

The women immediately got into their cars and left. As they crossed over a bridge, they realized the urgency of the situation when the raging waters cascading down the mountain washed away the bridge they had just driven over! Continuing on, the women traveled to a fork in the road, got out of their cars, asked for directions, jumped back into the cars, and drove on.

Ney Bailey's car went one way, and another car went a different way. Tragically, the seven women in the other car drowned. Not knowing of her friends' deaths, Ney and her companions huddled together in prayer once their car reached higher ground. With the authority of Scripture undergirding her, she began praying, "Lord, Your Word says, 'In everything give thanks, because this is the will of God in Christ Jesus concerning us.' So while we are in this, we choose with our wills to thank You.

"And, Lord, Your Word says, 'All things'—including this— 'work together for good to those who love You'—and we do—'and are called according to Your purpose'—and we are.

"You have also said that heaven and earth will pass away before Your Word passes away. So Your Word is truer than anything we are feeling or experiencing right now."[1]

Praying God's Word

Faith is not a feeling, and Ney lived out that truth in the situation I just described. Despite whatever she was feeling— panic, fear, worry—Ney chose to put her faith in God and the truths of His Word and not in her feelings. As her prayer reveals, she turned to God and clung to the promises found in His Word when her feelings and thoughts might have run wild. Ney Bailey's prayer taught me three lessons I have tried to apply in my own Christian life.

First, *pray "Your Word says..."*—Ney showed me how to pray using the authority of Scripture. I saw right away the value of praying "Your Word says...," of letting God's truths guide my petitions. Now, whenever I counsel a woman who needs help praying about difficult issues, I share Ney's prayer with her and tell her to pray God's Word.

Second, *pray the truth of Romans 8:28*—Ney's prayer taught me how to use the truth of Romans 8:28 concerning my life. Following her model, I now pray, "God, Your Word says 'all things'—including this _____ (and I fill in the blank, naming my present problem)— 'work together for good.'" The simple exercise of "filling in the blank" forces me to acknowledge God's involvement in my life and reminds me that He is the source of my strength and hope.

Third, *pray to be faith oriented*—This prayer taught me that I can never view my life through the lens of feelings. They are too varied and unstable! No, I must be faith oriented rather than feeling oriented. Faith is not a feeling. Faith looks to God and trusts Him to work out the present difficulty for His purposes and my good. I must look to God and to His Word—and to Romans 8:28!—and I must remember that He will indeed work all things for my good!

As we're continuing to learn, God is in complete control of every aspect of our lives. Furthermore, He promises to work "all things" for our good and His purposes. We can definitely have hope in Him and put our God-given faith in Him.

Trusting God's Good Purpose

In His promise of Romans 8:28, God gives us glorious good news! He reassures us that His purposes for us are good. The words are straightforward—"We know that all things work together for good." This truth assures us that the end result of all that God allows to touch our lives will be good. You see, He is working *all* things (no disclaimers or fine print here!) together for good. When we choose to believe this truth, we can't help but find hope in God as we trust in His good purpose for whatever life holds.

Joseph saw God's good purpose—In this book we have already met Joseph, a person who found hope in God despite the twists and turns his life took (Genesis 37–50). As the favored son of Jacob, Joseph found himself in great disfavor with his brothers. Acting out of hatred and envy, the brothers plotted Joseph's murder. However, at the last moment they sold him into slavery instead.

Joseph ended up in Egypt as a slave to Potiphar, the captain of Pharaoh's bodyguard. Because Joseph was greatly blessed by God, he rose to a powerful position of status within the Egyptian government (Genesis 39:2-3). Then, when famine struck Joseph's homeland, his brothers— the ones who had disrupted his life and brought on unmeasurable pain and torment—suddenly appeared before him in Egypt, asking *him* for food to stay alive!

Now it was decision-making time for Joseph. He had a serious choice to make. He could fill his brothers' grain sacks with life-giving food...or he could have his brothers killed (either directly by an order or indirectly by with-holding the grain). As a man of God, Joseph extended grace to his brothers, saying, "As for you, you meant evil against me; but *God meant it for good,* in order to bring it about as it is this day, to save many people alive" (Genesis 50:20).

At this point in time—after being rejected, mistreated, sold into slavery, falsely accused, imprisoned, forgotten, and finally blessed—Joseph saw that God had indeed been at work all along. Joseph, therefore, found no reason to place blame on his brothers...or God(!), or to feel bitter against them...or God! As writer Chuck Swindoll puts it, by choosing to see Jehovah at work, Joseph...

> ...blazes a new trail through a jungle of mistreat-ment, false accusations, undeserved punishment, and gross misunderstanding. He exemplifies for-giveness, freedom from bitterness, and an unbe-lievably positive attitude toward those who had done him harm.[2]

You must trust in God's good purpose—Are you like me? It's soooo easy to let myself get bogged down in the tiny details of my own experience. I tend to spend a lot of time and energy sorting out how I feel about a problem, ana-lyzing my emotions, deciding what I like or don't like about the situation, evaluating the pain on a scale of one to ten, and choosing to worry, blame, rant and rave, or sink into depression. I even try to figure out how I'm going to make the situation better...or get myself out of it!

But I can tell you, this kind of introspection and focus on self hardly leads to hope...or victory...or greater faith. But I'm learning! Now (well, most of the time, anyway), instead of asking, "What does this mean to me?" I'm learning to ask, "What does this mean to God?" Posing this kind of question points me to God and His perspective. And it will do the same for you.

And let me encourage you! Although trials hurt terribly, you can count on the end being good. Why? Because God Himself is good. In Matthew 7:9-10, Jesus asks, "What man is there among you who, if his son asks for bread, will give him a stone? Or if he asks for a fish, will give him a serpent?" Then, to answer His questions, Christ states this fact about God, the Father: "If you then, being evil, know how to give good gifts to your children, how much more will your Father who is in heaven give good things to those who ask Him!" (Matthew 7:11).

Sometimes what God has given you may look and feel like a stone or a snake. But your heart and mind must believe and trust that your heavenly Father, our good God, is working those things out for your good and according to His good purpose. Look at your life situation. Then look at your powerful and redemptive God and at the promise of Romans 8:28. When you do, you have another decision to make—a decision of faith—to put your trust in God and believe that the end will be good, regardless of how life looks or feels in the present. This is how you love God with all your mind. By faith, decide to trust God for the ultimate purpose He is working in your life.

The promise of Romans 8:28 serves as a lens through which you (and I) can have a godly perspective on your life, from birth to death. Because of the words in this scripture, you can know that your good God is working the miracle of using the bad—*every*thing, from the most minor of incidents to the greatest of tragedies—for good. Counting on the fact that the end of all things will be good gives you hope. It also helps you to be faith oriented—not feeling oriented—about your present pain. After all, feelings distort your vision. And today's obstacles often prevent a hopeful and faith-filled view of the end. But by responding to God's love, by loving Him with all your mind and trusting in Him, you will be blessed with hope in His promise that He works in everything to bring about what is good.

Giving God Our Love

Before we finish this chapter about God's glorious goodness and His marvelous, unmerited love for us, we must examine our love for Him. Look again at Romans 8:28. We know that God causes all things to work together for good *"to those who love God...."* The words "to those who love God" are important because the promise of Romans 8:28 is not for everybody. It can be claimed only by those who love God.

How do we show God our love for Him? Christ answered this question in just seven words: "If you love Me, keep My commandments" (John 14:15). Another version of the Bible succinctly says, "If you love me, obey me."[3]

It's obvious that our love for God is measured by our obedience. So take a few minutes—now and regularly—to look at your life and evaluate how closely you are following God. When I do this, I take a pen and paper and run a check of the elements of my entire life. I ask myself,

"Is there anything wrong in my relationship with God?" and I write down my answer. I then ask the same question regarding my husband, my children, my parents, my in-laws, my siblings, my home, my spiritual and personal growth, my areas of service to the Lord, and my relationships with other people. I write down whatever comes to my mind and then have a time of prayer. I spend time asking God's forgiveness for where I have been disobedient, unloving, or unfaithful. As 1 John 1:9 tells us, whenever we confess our sins, our good God "is faithful and just to forgive us our sins and to cleanse us from all unrighteousness."

You might want to take some time each day (perhaps during your regular prayer time) to mentally examine the priority areas of your life. Evaluate your relationship with God and with your family members, how things are at home, your spiritual growth, the challenges you face as you serve God, the demands of the workplace, and your involvement with people. Look for areas where you have not obeyed God and His Word. Then purpose to give God greater devotion and obedience...to love Him.

Loving God...Even More

*H*ow can you love God...even more? Because we demonstrate our love for God by obeying Him, it helps to begin each day by purposing to follow His ways all day long. My first-thing-in-the-morning prayer is that I will make His choices and do His will with each thought, word, and deed throughout the day. This prayer helps keep me on my toes and keeps me aware of Him as I go about my day meeting people, doing the tasks at hand, and facing any challenges along the way.

And I pray this prayer again whenever the phone rings or I meet someone I know. I ask God to help me say the right words and do the right thing. For example, if the person who calls is upset, I pray, "Please, God, let me respond in Your way....Help me stay calm....Help me know when to speak and when to only listen....Help me to help."

God works for good all of the things that happen to those who love Him, and we love God by obeying Him. So, dear reader, what is your current level of obedience to the God who loves you and whom you desire to love...even more? How warm is your love for God? Is it red-hot and pure...lukewarm and indifferent...or ice-cold, below freezing? A pure and hot love for God is truly a well-spring of hope in Him!

20

$\mathcal{N}$AVIGATING THE
MAZE OF LIFE

❦

We know that all things work together
for good to those who love God,
to those who are called
according to His purpose.

ROMANS 8:28

$\mathcal{I}$ REMEMBER WHEN MY LIFE had no purpose. As an average woman with an average marriage, two average preschool daughters, and an average house, I shook my fist at the kitchen ceiling one average and desperate day and cried, "There has to be more to life than this!"

I was hopeless! After all, where could I find hope when I hadn't even found the purpose behind the things I was doing? My lack of purpose caused me to wonder, to doubt, and to rage. But, praise God, He used my search for purpose to help me recognize that I needed Jesus Christ! By following the path He led me on to discover Jesus Christ, and by walking through the circumstances He created, I acted on that need. I became a Christian several months later.

And suddenly I saw the purpose of everything in my life because I saw that God had a purpose for me!

Knowing that God has a purpose for my life and for my salvation brings me great joy and hope. But it also brings with it great responsibility. You see, now that I know there is a use and a reason for my life...and days...and minutes, I also know I can no longer live my life according to my own desires, plans, dreams, or whims. I am to live totally for God's purposes. Therefore, I am not to make decisions based on pleasing people. No, I must please God! You see, I exist to serve Him and His people according to the gifts He has given me and in the situations where He places me.

Discovering God's Purpose

Do you ever have what I call doubtful days—days when the dull routine of duty weighs you down? Or days when the curveballs of surprise, disappointment, and tragedy leave you feeling like you're striking out? Well, there's good news for both of us! The constant awareness that God has a purpose for us gives us great hope when the day-to-day practicalities and challenges discourage and bewilder us.

Imagine a maze in an English garden. These intriguing puzzles, created by six- or seven-foot hedges, were used initially to provide people with some entertaining exercise after their meals. The diners would enter the confusing and baffling network of shrubs and try to find their way to the pleasant place in the center of the maze where there was usually a tree, some flowering plants, and a garden seat where they could sit, relax, and visit...before trying to find their way out.

One evening as I looked at pictures of these garden mazes in a coffee-table book at a friend's home, I thought, *Why, this is the way life is!* We follow along the maze of life, randomly making turns and choosing our paths.

Then we come to know Christ as our Lord and Savior. From that point on, we have purpose—to serve God. We're still traversing the maze of life, but now we have direction. God keeps us moving forward as we pray and dedicate our lives to serving Him, becoming more Christlike, and spreading the gospel. As we begin to grow and move along in our Christian life, we come to corners...special moments when God guides our lives into new directions or deeper understandings of His purpose for us. And off we go, following God's will on the new path! Unfortunately, sometimes we stray from God's will or misunderstand His direction and come to dead ends. Then, through further prayer, we take action and seek the Lord for clarification or new guidance...and set off accordingly.

While we're in the maze, we never know who or what we'll encounter. Why, we don't even know exactly where we're going! But we do know that we are to keep moving. And as we continue on according to God's will and His leading, He fulfills His purpose for us. God doesn't ask us to understand the twists and turns, the why's and the how's of life. He asks only that we trust that He is working His purpose in us as we live out our purpose of serving Him.

And now we're right back to the incredible promise of Romans 8:28! We know God has a purpose for us. That's yet another sparkling reason why we can have joy and hope in Him each day...no matter what happens in that day. And knowing that God has a purpose for us makes every day significant.

Finding God's Will

As you know, trying to determine God's will and specific purposes for us is not always easy. The apostle Paul knew this all too well! In Acts 16:6-10, we learn something about how God reveals His will to His people. In this passage, Luke, the writer of Acts, is reporting on Paul's second missionary journey.

> Now when they had gone through Phrygia and the region of Galatia, they were forbidden by the Holy Spirit to preach the word in Asia. After they had come to Mysia, they tried to go into Bithynia, but the Spirit did not permit them. So passing by Mysia, they came down to Troas. And a vision appeared to Paul in the night. A man of Macedonia stood and pleaded with him, saying, "Come over to Macedonia and help us." Now after he had seen the vision, immediately we sought to go to Macedonia, concluding that the Lord had called us to preach the gospel to them.

How were things going on that missions endeavor? The faithful apostle was busy fulfilling God's purpose for his life every single day by proclaiming the gospel. But then look what happened! After preaching in one area of Asia Minor, Paul decided to travel in another direction...but was "*forbidden* by the Holy Spirit to preach the word in Asia"!

So what did Paul do? How did he respond to "a shut door"? Did he stop, quit, turn toward home, and turn in his apostle's badge? Did he have a fit, explode, rant and rave? Did he complain, pout and sulk, sink into a depression? After all, all he was trying to do was obediently and faithfully fulfill his commission and calling to preach the gospel!

No, Paul kept moving. With that direction blocked, Paul simply turned another way, toward Bithynia. However, once again, "the Spirit *did not permit* them." Again, what did Paul do? Did he stop, quit, turn in his apostle's badge...have a fit, explode, rant and rave...complain, pout and sulk, sink into a depression?

No, Paul kept moving. With only one possibility remaining, Paul headed in that direction, toward Troas. And when he did so, "a vision appeared to Paul in the night. A man of Macedonia stood and pleaded with him, saying, 'Come over to Macedonia and help us.'" And Paul and the people traveling with him immediately went to Macedonia to preach the gospel to them.

And the marvelous result? God's purpose? God's plan? The reason for all of the twists and turns, obstacles, and blocked efforts? Paul's response to God's leading in Asia Minor led to the birth of the church at Philippi...in what is now modern Greece!

Discovering God's Purpose...for You!

When you, like Paul, seek to know God's will and to be used for His ultimate purposes, God will guide you, as He did the apostle, through the maze of life. Although Luke does not say in Acts exactly how God "forbade" or refused to "permit" Paul to go in certain directions, the passage does teach us that we can trust God to close doors and block our paths in order to keep us going where He wants us to go.

My friend, our role is to love God and keep moving through life according to His purpose for us. His role is to lead us in the maze so that we can fulfill the specific purposes He calls us to at the same time that He fulfills His purpose in and through us. And God uses people, events, and circumstances, both good and bad, to move us ultimately toward the fulfillment of His will and purpose for our lives.

Exactly what is God's purpose for us, His children? As Paul explains in Romans 8:29, the primary purpose of "all things" in our lives is Christlikeness: "For whom He foreknew, He also predestined to be conformed to the image of His Son." Everything—every person, every event—that touches us is for the purpose of making us like Christ. We can find comfort and hope as we navigate the maze of life when we remember the fact that God will use whatever He permits to happen to us to fulfill His purposes *and* to make us more like Jesus.

Minister and author Alan Redpath writes this about the promise of Romans 8:28 and 29:

> There is nothing—no circumstance, no trouble, no testing—that can ever touch me until, first of all it has gone past God and past Christ, right through to me. If it has come that far, it has come with a *great purpose,* which I may not understand at the moment. But as I *refuse* to become panicky, as I lift up my eyes to him and accept it as coming from the throne of God for some *great purpose of blessing* to my own heart, no sorrow will ever disturb me, no trial will ever disarm me, no circumstance will cause me to fret—for I *shall rest in the joy of what my Lord is*—That is the rest of victory.[1]

The truth of Romans 8:28 should cause us to rest in the Lord and wait patiently for Him (Psalm 37:7)—for Him to act, for Him to work, for Him to save (if that is His will), for Him to reveal His purposes. Even if we never know why things happen, we can still rest in God, hope in Him, and believe that He is using every aspect of our lives to make us more like Jesus.

One woman in particular shows Christians how to live with hope in God, trusting His goodness...and His purpose. A striking example of faith, this woman loved God and trusted His purposes for her despite tragedy, hardship, and suffering.

God's Songbird

Fanny Crosby, the famous hymn writer, was a woman who believed that God's purposes are good and who clearly heard His calling on her life. You can sense this in her comments about the doctor who caused her blindness: "I have heard that this physician never ceased expressing his regret at the occurrence; and that it was one of the sorrows of his life. But if I could meet him now, I would say, 'Thank you, thank you, over and over again for making me blind.'...Although it may have been a blunder on the physician's part, it was no mistake on God's. I verily believe it was His intention that I should live my days in physical darkness, so as to be better prepared to sing His praises and incite others to do so."[2] Through a doctor's apparent mistake, God gave to the church the wonderful songs of a blind Fanny Crosby who, with her increased spiritual insight, wrote hymns until she died at age 95—hymns that have endured and inspired others to greater faith.

When has someone else's "blunder" or "mistake" touched your life? Or when has someone's malice severely impacted you? People who have faith in God and hope in

Him accept such unexplainable events as "no mistake on God's part." They know that every event involves "His intention" and leads them one step closer to discovering and fulfilling God's purpose. They look to the God they trust and love for strength and let His ability transform their disabilities.

Fanny Crosby found some of her options for life eliminated as she navigated the maze of her life. But, with God's blessing, she also discovered a uniquely personal way—God's will and purpose for her—to serve Him and His people. Fanny Crosby couldn't see, but she could sing and write poems. After a doctor's "mistake," she gave to God what she had—her singing and her writing—and He used her greatly for His kingdom. She became God's songbird.

Loving God...Even More

Like Fanny Crosby, a Christian who experienced tragedy in her life and continued to love God, you can model a strong trust and hope in God despite the events you encounter as you navigate the maze of life. So to start—or continue—down the path of loving God even more, pray and think through these exercises.

First, take an inventory of your life. Chart the path you've walked, and review how God has shown you His will through the years. When did He stop you, turn you, send you back, or direct you in another way? How did God change your direction? Did He "forbid" something? Did He "fail to permit" something? Was there an "accident" or a "mistake" along the way, a tragedy, an unjust slander, an envious person, a failure, a lack, a handicap, an oversight, a deep hurt in your past?

Now look again at the autobiography you have just sketched. Where has God worked bad for good? And where do you see Him making you more like Christ? As you recognize God's unseen involvement along the way, you may now pray the love-filled prayer Ney Bailey taught us: "Lord, Your Word says 'All things—including this (fill in the blank) _____ —work together for good to those who love You'...and I do." You can even thank God for His wisdom and ways, as unsearchable as they may sometimes be.

As you consider your autobiography you'll be able to see that it is in limiting that God reveals the limitlessness of His power and grace and purposes. In God's maze, God's "no" to one thing is "yes" to another. "No" in one direction is a clear indicator of "yes" in a different direction. "No" to certain pursuits only means "yes" to others. With God as your guide in the maze of life, a "no" is never the end. A negative is never permanent.

And even in the darkness that comes when we are unable to see how anything good could possibly come out of the bad, God's promise in Romans 8:28 offers us the light of hope. In fact, Romans 8:28 serves as a rainbow, brilliantly and miraculously arching through the dark clouds and mist that may hang over the maze of life, bringing the hope of God's promise that He, ever faithful to His promise, works all things together for good for those who love Him...and we do!

Living Out God's Plan

❦

*For I know the thoughts I think
toward you, says the LORD,
thoughts of peace and not of evil,
to give you a future and a hope.*

JEREMIAH 29:11

21

$\mathscr{E}$NDURING
DIFFICULT TIMES

❦

"For I know the thoughts that I think
toward you," says the LORD....

JEREMIAH 29:11

$\mathscr{W}$HEN MY FRIEND JUDY MOVED from Missouri to California, she brought her country upbringing with her and began to create a country-style home for her family out West. During the 25 years she has lived in her house, she has worked steadily on her dream of living in a country cottage. In time, when she was satisfied with the inside of her home, Judy went to work on her porch. There you'll find a cozy tea table and chairs surrounded by a wooden bench, a bird cage, several birdhouses, baskets full of plants and old wooden-handled gardening tools. A padded lounge chair, an old wicker rocker, and a low table arranged around a braided rug invite you to relax. Tea on Judy's porch is quite a special treat!

With the porch complete, Judy began working on her garden. A step off the porch puts you on a walkway that leads you to the left, where wooden rails set off a U-shaped flower bed. There, flowering vines wrap around a trellis, the porch posts, and the rails. Stepping-stones take you to trimmed trees, where bountiful Boston ferns hang from low branches. Flowers have been carefully planted so all the brilliant colors can be seen and enjoyed, and creeping figs happily embrace the aged wooden fence. Judy's garden is a gracious place of peace and beauty.

One evening, as our family visited with Judy and her family, my husband said, "Judy, this is a beautiful garden, but...what happened over there?" Jim was pointing to a rock pile at the border of Judy's garden. Next to the rocks was a woodpile, a tree stump, a dead tree, some gravel, and an assortment of discarded flowerpots. The area spoke of barrenness and neglect.

But Judy said, "Oh, I have a plan!" And glad to have an interested audience, she grabbed a bulging manila file folder. Spilling out of it were newspaper clippings, magazine articles, gardening tips, pictures of other gardens, instructions for choosing year-round plants, and her drawings and sketches. For years, Judy had been collecting ideas and planning her ideal garden, and she was excited about her plan. "Oh, I have a plan!"

God Has a Plan for You

"Oh, I have a plan!" is exactly what God is telling the Israelites in Jeremiah 29:11. To the children of Israel who had been uprooted from their homes and carried away as captives to Babylon—and to you and me as well—God declares, "I know the thoughts that I think toward you... thoughts of peace and not of evil, to give you a future and a hope." As another translation of the Bible puts it, "'I know the plans that I have for you,' declares the LORD, 'plans for welfare and not for calamity to give you a future and a hope'" (NASB).

Although the heartbroken prophet Jeremiah prophesied doom for these stiff-necked people who had turned away from God, he also preached hope to these captives—hope that was based on the promise God made to them as recorded in Jeremiah 29:11. Having announced their sentence of 70 years of bondage in Babylon, Jeremiah then told these displaced Jews how to survive those years.

And here's good news! Jeremiah's words of instruction and "how-to's" can help us, too, when we find ourselves enduring difficult times in places or predicaments we didn't choose for ourselves. To remind yourself of God's message to your heart during hard and difficult times, take to heart —and to memory!—these ABCs.

A — Acknowledge God's Hand

According to Jeremiah, we need to first recognize God's hand in whatever has happened. Speaking through Jeremiah, God told the Israelites four times, "*I* have caused you to be carried away from Jerusalem to Babylon...captive" (Jeremiah 29:4,7,14,20). God explained that it wasn't the Babylonians alone who had taken them away from their homeland and into exile. No, God Himself had allowed it. Likewise, whatever circumstances you and I find ourselves in, we need to remember that God has allowed us to be there. We may wonder, "What happened?" and the situation may not be our ideal, but it is in God's hands. Your life is *not* out of control! And nothing has just randomly "happened" to put you where you are.

And the result? We can better endure difficult times when we acknowledge that God is indeed in full control of not only the universe but of our circumstances. Thinking the truth about God and our circumstances can help eliminate insecurity, bewilderment, blaming, and bitterness. We can then enjoy greater peace...*in* our trying situations.

B — Bloom Where You Are Planted

We are to "bloom and grow" where we are planted. What does this mean? We are to go on loving the Lord with our whole being—heart, soul, strength, and mind. And we are to go on fulfilling His purposes for us wherever we find ourselves—no matter how undesirable or unexpected our circumstances. The prophet Jeremiah told the crushed and bewildered people of Israel exactly how to live during their exile. He said (and pay special attention to the verbs), "Build houses and dwell in them; plant gardens and eat their fruit. Take wives and beget sons and daughters; and take wives for your sons and give your daughters to husbands, so that they may bear sons and daughters—that you may be increased there, and not diminished" (Jeremiah 29:5-6).

The priorities of building solid, long-lasting, and ongoing marriages, families, and home lives were to be their focus—not their pain. Captivity for God's people was true and real. God, in essence, said, "You're going to be here a while. This is not temporary. This is not a short-term captivity. So have something to show for it! Focus your energies on something positive—your growth and betterment."

God called the captives to make homes, plant crops, and bear fruit in the land of their affliction. Life was to go on for them. And life is to go on for you and me, too, in our afflictions. Whatever sorrow or situation we may be facing—when we wonder, *What happened over there?* God wants us to continue building where we are and blooming where we're planted. That's how we endure difficult times.

Jeremiah's "how-to" was this: "Keep on keeping on! Keep on building! Keep on functioning! Keep on planting! Live! Bloom! Grow! Increase! Don't merely sit around being sad or depressed, waiting for things to change or get better. *Make* things better!"

C — *Concentrate on God's Promises*

On the heels of Jeremiah's specific instructions to the Israelites came his pronouncement of God's promise of a return to their homeland:

> After seventy years are completed at Babylon, I will visit you and perform My good word toward you, and cause you to return to this place.... I will bring you back from your captivity; I will gather you from all the nations and from all the places where I have driven you...and I will bring you to the place from which I cause you to be carried away captive (29:10,14).

In the meantime, God comforted His children with these words: "I know the thoughts that I think toward you... thoughts of peace and not of evil, to give you a future and a hope."

Whenever these misplaced people were discouraged, they were to find their hope and strength to endure in *God* and in *His promises*...and so are we. The plans God has for us—plans for welfare and not for calamity, for good and not for evil, to give us a future and a hope—are a source of real confidence and assurance, no matter what challenges, hurts, and questions we face along the way.

Where do you tend to focus your attention when things fall apart, when you wonder, *What happened over there?* No matter what is occurring in your life, concentrate on God's promises. They assure you over and over again of the nature and reality of God and His character. Through them you will never lose sight of the bright hope of your future! You can have glorious hope even when life looks hopeless.

D — Do Something Useful

While you are *in* your difficult times, ever-confident in God's promised outcome for your trials, you can "do something useful." Wherever you are (which is where God has sovereignly placed you!), you can serve God, your family, and His people. Sure, there are a lot of things you don't know about your present condition, but one thing you do know is that God calls us to serve Him and His people (Matthew 20:26-28). So serve away! Roll up your sleeves and serve God and others in the present, even *in* your hard times.

In fact, this is the message Jeremiah delivered to the captive Israelites who are having their first taste of the bitterness of exile. As we've seen, Jeremiah was specific about how the Israelites were to endure their hard years of exile. "The captives in Babylon were to settle down and live as normally as possible under the circumstances (build houses, marry, multiply...and pray)."[1] In other words, the children of Israel were to do something useful. They were to serve God in their marriages, their families, their community, and their businesses. Such effort and usefulness would help ward off depression and discouragement and give each day purpose and fulfillment.

That's our assignment, too. Wherever we are and however good or bad our circumstances are, if we are married, God calls us to serve our spouses. And if we are parents, we are to nurture and love our children (Ephesians 6:4 and Titus 2:4). And each of us—married or single—is also called to serve the body of Christ, His church (1 Corinthians 12:7). Wherever we are and whatever our circumstances, we are to serve God. These roles require energy, self-sacrifice, and strength, but God graciously provides everything we need to do something useful...even in the midst of suffering.

These few lines of poetry express our assignment from God to do something useful...*while* we are in our troubles:

> We cannot see beyond the door,
> We know not what He hath in store...
>
> We can but bow our hearts and pray
> For strength to serve Him day by day.[2]

In our next chapter we'll witness some of God's people who, when they found themselves in hard and difficult places—places they didn't choose and places they didn't want to be in—followed God's plan for enduring difficult times. They...

A cknowledged God's hand,
B loomed where they were planted,
C oncentrated on God's promises, and
D id something useful.

You're in for a treat, as well as a large helping of encouragement!

Loving God...Even More

*A*nd now I want to bring our attention back to God. Remembering your gracious God and the promise of His good plan for you and focusing your thoughts on His purposes for your life can establish and anchor you and your emotions. It's also a way to love Him with all your mind. Panic, despair, nervousness, bewilderment, fear—God speaks against emotions like these in His Word. In fact, when the circumstances of life might lead to uncertainty and confusion, the bright promise of Jeremiah 29:11 gives us certainty, clarity, and hope.

My dear friend, God has a plan for your welfare! When you wonder and ask, *But...what happened over there?* He shouts back to you through Jeremiah 29:11, "Oh, I have a plan!" The path of your life may zig and zag, twist and turn, but God has promised you "a future and a hope."

With this promise you don't need to know the future! Instead, you can be content and at peace in knowing, trusting, and loving the Father, whose plans are for good and not evil. All will be well. You can be secure in that fact. It's His promise to you! Therefore, you can endure to the end of your difficult times. And you can build and bear fruit in the meantime.

22

$\mathscr{B}$EARING FRUIT
DURING DIFFICULT TIMES

∽∞∾

"For I know the plans that I have
for you," declares the LORD....

JEREMIAH 29:11 NASB

$\mathscr{W}$HEN IT COMES TO ENDURING TRIALS and difficult times,
the Bible tells us to "count it all joy" (James 1:2)! In fact, we
can even find lists of the benefits to be gained, blessings to
be enjoyed, and lessons to be learned in our trials. For
instance, James writes that "the testing of your faith pro-
duces patience" and to "let patience have its perfect work,
that you may be perfect and complete, lacking nothing"
(verses 3-4). If you are wondering how in the world this is
possible, be sure to remember what we've already learned
about enduring difficult times:

- We know that God is the author and the
  finisher of our lives. Therefore, we know
  that we can **A**-cknowledge God and His

sovereignty in whatever circumstances we
are *in* and wherever we are, as difficult and
as painful as it may be.

- We know we can, by God's grace, **B**-loom
  where we are planted and bear fruit—even
  much fruit—in "the land of our affliction,"
  in our situation of sorrow.

- We know we can **C**-oncentrate on God's
  powerful and reassuring promises *while* we
  are in our difficult times, and go ahead and
  plant and increase because we know God
  will bring all good things to pass.

- We know that we are to **D**-o something
  useful, wherever we are, no matter how
  distressing the situation is.

Learning from God's Servants

When we look to the Bible and to believers who have
gone before us, we find inspiring examples of people who
served God wholeheartedly by doing something useful
while they were in difficult times and places.

Joseph — Think again on Joseph's life. He served God as
a slave, as a prisoner, and finally as an elevated official in
the Egyptian government. He served God as the trusted
manager of Potiphar's luxurious palace...as well as from a
dark, dank dungeon where he was in irons and his feet
were fastened with shackles (Psalm 105:18). Finally
released from prison after three years of unjust punish-
ment, Joseph became second in command in Egypt. In this
position, his service extended beyond that country's

boundaries to the entire known world as he dispensed life-giving grain during a serious famine.

Joseph suffered betrayal by his brothers, separation from his father and family, condemnation and imprisonment because of a false accusation, and unjust treatment. But Joseph served...no matter where he was...no matter what his situation...no matter who needed his service. He kept "many people alive" (Genesis 50:20) and bettered the lives of countless others. Only in the naming of Joseph's two sons do we sense his sorrow. "Joseph called the name of the first-born Manasseh: 'For God has made me forget all my toil and all my father's house.' And the name of the second he called Ephraim: 'For God has caused me to be fruitful in the land of my affliction'" (41:51-52).

Paul—The apostle Paul also models ongoing service to God...no matter what or where! Whether he was standing on the heights of Mars Hill debating with the best minds from the highest court of Athens or chained to a single guard in the depths of a dungeon, Paul served his Lord and His causes as a preacher of the gospel. Despite beatings, stonings, death threats, imprisonments, and various other forms of suffering, Paul kept on preaching (2 Corinthians 11:23-33).

How did Paul do it? How did he maintain his energy and zeal? We have already discovered his secret: Paul focused on the object of his love—the Lord Jesus Christ—and kept on keeping on, even through pain. He declared, "Forgetting those things which are behind and reaching forward to those things which are ahead, I press toward the goal for the prize of the upward call of God in Christ Jesus" (Philippians 3:13-14). Paul desired to be useful to his Lord day by day, wherever he was, and whatever his condition.

Madame Guyon—In the eighteenth century, Jeanne Marie Guyon was imprisoned in the Bastille (described by some as the most horrible prison on earth). Madame Guyon spent four of her seven years there in solitary confinement. While serving her sentence, she focused her thoughts on God. It was there she wrote—

> A little bird I am,
> Shut from the fields of air;
> And in my cage I sit and sing
> To Him who placed me there;
> Well pleased a prisoner to be,
> Because, my God, it pleased Thee.[1]

The result of Madame Guyon's time—the fruit she bore while in prison—was her writing. She wrote many books, including a 20-volume commentary on the Bible.[2]

Mrs. Studd—In more recent times, Mrs. C.T. Studd shows us service in every circumstance. She served her missionary husband as his wife and manager. However, as she grew increasingly ill and even as an invalid, Mrs. Studd continued to serve her husband and God's people. "She had to go to her room each night at seven and not come down the next day till lunch time....From her bed and invalid couch she formed Prayer Centres, issued monthly pamphlets by the thousand, wrote often twenty to thirty letters a day, planned and edited the first issues of the *Heart of Africa Mission Magazine*."[3] Mrs. Studd served in sickness as well as in health, bearing fresh fruit in her illness and affliction.

Hudson Taylor—Missions founder Hudson Taylor also served God wherever he was. When illness forced him to leave his ministry in China and return to England, he used this "downtime" to found the China Inland Mission. When he returned to China, he had created a mission organization to support him and had recruited new missionaries to accompany him.[4]

As the man who advocated, "Do small things as if they were great, because of the majesty of Jesus Christ,"[5] Hudson Taylor's "small things" went on to add up to great things as he sought to do something useful...no matter what.

And he suffered! Mr. Taylor suffered physically from illness, was persecuted and attacked in China, had his house set on fire, lost his wife and two children on the mission field in a raging cholera epidemic. Yet he kept on serving, laboring, and praying...and believing "God himself is at the helm, ordering all things after the counsel of his own will. He has a plan and he is carrying it out; he has a throne and that throne rules over all."[6]

Like the examples I've mentioned—and countless others I could list—you and I can and are to serve God...no matter what our circumstances. He calls us to serve Him and, through the prophet Jeremiah's words to suffering captives in Jeremiah 29, God calls us to serve Him even when we're not where we want to be and when life is not easy. Despite their Babylonian exile, the children of Israel were to keep living for God, serving God, and praying to God...and so are we.

As one Bible commentator observes, "Life cannot grind to a halt during troubled times. In an unpleasant or distressing situation, we must adjust and keep moving.... When you enter times of trouble or sudden change, pray diligently and move ahead, doing whatever you can rather than giving up because of uncertainty."[7] Put simply, we are to serve God—no matter what. That's a part of His "plan" for us.

Doing God's Will

As followers of Christ, we want to serve Him through the thick and the thin, the good times and the bad, in the best of days and in the difficult times. Our heart's desire is to live out His plan and purpose for us...to bear fruit that glorifies our Lord. But what is His will? And how can we find it so we can do it?

We know that we can search for God's will, pray to discover it, even fast for greater spiritual discernment to perceive God's direction. But here's one aspect of God's will we don't need to look for: His will is for us to serve Him at *all times*, in *all places*, and in *all situations*. And closeness to God gives us greater sensitivity to Him and to what His plans for us are. So to discern God's plan—His will—and to live it out requires that we nurture our relationship to God.

Here are three tried-and-true ways to discover God's will for you and to follow His plan so that you become a masterpiece—*His* masterpiece!

1. *Delight yourself in God*—Consider this truth: "*Delight* yourself also in the LORD; and He shall give you the desires of your heart" (Psalm 37:4). To delight yourself in the Lord means to seek your pleasure in Him, to make Him your true joy,[8] to "indulge thyself in the Lord."[9] When you "delight yourself in the Lord," God, His Word, and His ways become the focus and foundation of your life. He becomes what matters most to you.

And the blessed result? "He shall give you the desires of your heart." God puts His desires into your heart. His desires will actually become your desires, and your desires will be His. You won't know where one leaves off and the other begins because you will be delighting in Him to the point that you are adopting His thoughts and His ways. His plans are becoming your plans and your plans are becoming His!

2. *Indulge yourself in God's Word*—Have you ever noticed that the more you are with someone, the more you become like that person? Maybe you've noticed that you and your spouse or best friend use the same figures of speech and share many of the same opinions and perspectives on life. Or maybe you've been surprised to see your children reflect your attitudes and mannerisms! That's because the more we are with someone, the more we tend to become like that person.

This same principle holds true when it comes to indulging in God's Word. The more time you spend reading and studying the Bible, the more you resemble God. You will begin to think as God thinks and desire what He desires, which leads to Christlike behavior.

3. *Commit yourself to the Lord*— Psalm 37:5 says, "Commit your way to the LORD, trust also in Him, and He shall bring it to pass." In other words, commit yourself and your activities to the Lord. This involves the complete commitment of your life. A paraphrase of this promise could read, "Trust God to take over your career, home, work, all the circumstances, aims, and ambitions of life, and He will so mould events that your deepest and purest desires shall find unmeasured fulfillment and life will be filled with utter

satisfaction."[10] What a promise! What hope! What a plan God has for us, His children!

Delighting in the Lord, knowing His Word, and committing yourself to the Lord are ways to ensure that your plans and desires for yourself match God's plans.

Loving God...Even More

So now the questions is, How can we love God...even more? How can we tap into His amazing, all-sufficient grace and strength so that we can endure our difficult times and bear His beautiful fruit during them, so that we can become His masterpiece?

Start here: Put God first each day. Delight in Him...first and foremost! Make it a habit not to turn on the television or radio or read the newspaper before you spend some time reading His Word. Delighting yourself in the Lord means choosing Him each day, and that means choosing to make more time for His Word than any other kind of input.

Next, indulge yourself in God's Word. If you're spending five minutes with the Bible and five hours taking in TV programs, beware! Your values, standards, and views on life, marriage, and the world will probably not be God's!

And finally, commit yourself and every aspect of your life to God. When you do, you'll find your thoughts, plans, and activities established and blessed. In prayer, commit each fresh new day to God and dedicate it to Him. That's how you love Him. Then He can direct your thoughts, plans, dreams, and acts for the rest of the day.

Delighting in the Lord, indulging in His Word, and committing ourselves to Him are sure ways we can love God each day. These ways of loving God also enable us to serve Him better because they bring us closer to Him. And serving God—no matter what has happened or is happening—is part of His plan for us.

Dear reading friend, regardless of where you have been placed by God, and regardless of your difficult times, you my friend can acknowledge and worship God, remember His blessed promises, be useful to others, and bloom and bear fruit there. After all, just as my friend Judy was able to say about her garden, "Oh, I have a plan!" God is able to say about your life, "Oh, I have a plan!" What comfort and assurance, what hope and what security there is in the thought that God has a plan for us...a plan that will draw you closer to Him!

23

$\mathcal{B}$ECOMING
GOD'S MASTERPIECE

∽✖◦

"For I know the plans that I have for
you," declares the LORD, "plans for
welfare and not for calamity to give you
a future and a hope."

JEREMIAH 29:11 NASB

Learning to Look at God's Good Plan

As we've seen, God's timetable for the Israelites involved 70 years of captivity in Babylon (Jeremiah 29:10). Do you realize that 70 years was a death sentence for those who heard the prophet's words? God was letting them know they would die without ever seeing Jerusalem, their homeland, again. That's why it was urgent for them to plant and build, to focus on the next generation, because God's promise of peace and restoration would be fulfilled through the generations to come.

Imagine learning God's pronouncement that you would never again see your home again. It might be easy to feel that God was turning His back on you, that He no longer loved you, that He was no longer merciful or just. But, my friend, all these would be incorrect thoughts about God. To prevent such wrong thinking, God gave the Israelites— right on the heels of the 70-year sentence—the promise we've been looking at in this section about living out God's plan: "'For I know the thoughts that I think toward you,' says the LORD, 'thoughts of peace and not of evil, to give you a future and a hope'" (Jeremiah 29:11).

How were the sorrowing and suffering children of Israel to endure for 70 years? They would simply have to take God at His word. They would simply have to believe that He would not forget them...or His promise to them. They would have to count on His promise of a better future. For 70 years they would have to place their faith, hope, and trust in these words of assurance spoken to them by God through a prophet.

So far we've seen one reason why the words of Jeremiah offered all the security God's people, then and now, need: God has a plan for us. So, regardless of how your life may look or feel right this minute, take heart! Know that God is busy at work on His good plan for you. Remember, too, that His plan reflects His purposes, His methods, and His timetable...not yours. And never forget that while God is working out His plan in your life, painful as it may be at times, you are becoming His masterpiece!

God's Good Plan Is an Adventure

When my husband said, "Judy, this is a beautiful garden, but what happened over there?" Judy replied, "Oh, I have a plan!" Of course, Judy's plan was for beauty, order, and growth. She would never plan an ugly garden or one that couldn't flourish! Likewise, God would never plan a life for you of ugliness or barrenness, a life where you couldn't flourish in Him.

Let me ask you, Do the circumstances of your life seem overwhelming right now? Then try thinking about God's plan for your life as an adventure. This perspective can change your attitude as you realize that you are in something of "a secret conspiracy" with the Creator of the universe and the Author of your life. And what is the big secret? It's knowing that God has a plan, and His plan will end in good for you. These truths can put an adventuresome spin on the ups and downs, the twists and turns of the path that will eventually take you to God's good plan for you. So let your life be your personal adventure with God! And enjoy it!

Going on an adventure—The attitude that life in the Lord is an adventure certainly helped my friend Lauren and her mother deal with the events of a trip they took to Southern California some years ago. Here's what happened.

This adventuresome mother–daughter team drove down from Seattle to visit Lauren's sister in San Diego before attending a women's retreat at a church in Los Angeles.

While they were in San Diego, the Rodney King verdict was announced and rioting began in Los Angeles. The violence closed down businesses and freeways...and led to the cancellation of the retreat.

When Sunday morning arrived and the city was calm, Lauren decided they would drive several hours north to attend the worship service at a special church. After putting on their dresses and hose, she and her mom headed up the freeway...but somewhere along the way, they missed a freeway exit, and never made it to church.

So they decided to stay overnight with a friend in Los Angeles. When I finally heard they were nearby, I quickly invited them to have brunch with me the next morning... where they showed up wearing old, fading makeup and their Sunday church clothes, the only clothes they'd taken from San Diego! After a wonderful visit together, I walked them out to their car and hugged them goodbye when, as they drove away, I realized I hadn't given Lauren directions to the freeway, which had six freeway on-ramps and not one of them led to San Diego. Oh dear! They would be lost again! (And indeed they were, as I learned weeks later.)

Riding the roller coaster of life—How did they handle this trying trip, this comedy of obstacles and errors? Lauren and her mother actually *laughed* as we talked about it later! Nothing had bothered them. Why? Because they were on an adventure!

Their trip to Los Angeles had been one disaster and disappointment after another. No retreat, no refund, no Sunday-morning worship, no directions, and no clothes or makeup—and lost in L.A. twice! But their trust in God, whose plans are good and not evil, let them approach each event as part of an amazing adventure. They didn't get angry and frustrated because things didn't fit into their schedule or go as planned. They didn't complain, gripe, or get upset. Instead, they focused on the fact that God has a plan for their good. And that focus allowed them to view their obstacles, disappointments, and oversights as an incredible adventure rather than as fuel for frustration.

That's the power of God's promise and the truth in Jeremiah 29:11. Knowing about the end-result God promises invites us to accept the Christian life as an adventure. We can then ride the roller coaster of life, knowing God's plan is for our good.

God's Good Plan Is a Process

One reason many of us fail to enjoy the adventure of the Christian life is because it is a process. We like end results more than we like the process that gets us there. But between today and the good end that God promises, we have to go through a process.

Looking through the eyes of an artist—As the story goes, one day a colossal cube of marble was delivered to Michelangelo's art studio. He walked around it several times, at first surveying it from a step back, then looking at it closely. He touched it with his hands and even pressed his face against the cold block of stone. Suddenly he grabbed a mallet and a chisel and swung mightily. Blow after blow caused small chips of marble as well as large chunks to fly in every direction.

Watching in awe, his apprentice screamed above the noise of shattering stone, "What are you doing? You are ruining a perfect piece of marble!"

With the passion of an artist with a vision, Michelangelo answered, "I see an angel in there, and I've got to get him out!"

Looking through the eyes of the Master Artist—My friend, God looks at you with the same kind of eyes Michelangelo looked at the piece of marble. God sees in you the image of Christ, and He wants to set that beauty free. The "process" is freeing that "angel." In the words of Jeremiah, the process of life involves plans for good and "not of evil, to give you an expected end" (Jeremiah 29:11 KJV).

From time to time, you and I may—like Michelangelo's apprentice—cry out to God in bewilderment and terror, "What are You doing? You are ruining a perfect piece of marble!" Such a cry reveals our failure to understand the Artist, His vision, and the process of His work. God picks up His hammer and chisel and, acting out of His infinite love and wisdom, starts chipping away at the piece of marble that is our life. He carefully knocks off the unimportant, the meaningless, and the excess. His chisel cuts away the flaws and removes all that is ugly. While at times the process may be puzzling and even painful, we can be secure in the knowledge that it is for good, not evil. God wants to make us Christlike and perfect. He wants to make us His masterpiece!

Learning from the old masters—For a perspective on these puzzling and painful times, consider another example from the world of art. To give depth to a painting, Old World artists would first wash their white canvases with black. Only by beginning with that black could they later achieve the contrast, color, dimension, and depth they desired. After all, no painting is a masterpiece that possesses only one color or one intensity.

When the canvas of our life seems to be washed with black, we can remember the promise of Jeremiah 29:11, that the end will be good. We can let God's Word enable us to stand secure in the hope that when God completes His good plans, our lives will have greater depth, more interesting dimensions, and remarkable intensity.

God's Good Plan Is an Opportunity

The adventure of life is often difficult, and God's process in our lives may be quite painful at times. But it helps me to try to profit from every single experience that comes my way, the difficult and painful times as well as those times when life is going smoothly.

In her book *What Is a Family?* Edith Schaeffer advises that we treat adversity as an opportunity. She encourages us to regard hard times as important to our spiritual and personal growth, not merely as something we have to endure. She challenges us to make adversity count for something positive by learning all we can from it. And these words do not come glibly. Mrs. Schaeffer knows pain and adversity. Hear her words—those of a mother whose daughter suffered for two years with rheumatic fever and whose son was born with polio:

> For my own children I always tried to remind them to take the opportunity to get all the information and interesting facts they could, in the midst of their own times in hospitals...! "You may never have this chance again; find out all you can." Not only does it help to alleviate the fears and take minds off pain, but it is an honest fact that one may never have another chance to see certain things and to ask certain questions. "Now is your chance to find out all you can about a...hospital."—"Now is your chance to see how a blood transfusion works."—"Now you can read on that bottle what is mixed in the liquid they are about to put into you instead of food."—"See if you can look at the X-ray of that leg. Amazing the way a bone is apart!"[1]

Loving God...Even More

*D*ear reading friend, neither Edith Schaeffer nor I are encouraging you to downplay or look away from the hard times of life and the pain those times bring. Instead, our message is to look boldly into the face of adversity when it arrives and learn from it. Take it as an opportunity from God to learn something you might not learn otherwise.

Difficult times are opportunities that God promises to use—and is using—for our good. They are also exquisite opportunities to love God more. How? By encouraging you to believe in Him—in His good intentions, in His everlasting love, in His power, and in His promises, especially His promise to bring you to an expected end...to make you a masterpiece!

24

$\mathcal{L}$IVING OUT
GOD'S PROMISE

~∞~

*"For I know the plans that I have for
you," declares the* LORD, *"plans for
welfare and not for calamity to give you
a future and a hope."*

JEREMIAH 29:11 NASB

$\mathcal{A}$ PASTOR I KNOW HAS AN unbelievably positive attitude
toward life, come what may. In his position as a shepherd
to his flock, he has a lot of serious problems to sort
through and many heavy-duty counseling sessions to facil-
itate. And yet he has an incredible confidence in God's
process of working in His people's lives through such troubles. So, whenever someone approaches Jerry with a difficult or perplexing problem, he puts a note in a file folder
he has labeled "Wait a Week." During that week, Jerry
prays over every situation he's filed away. At the end of a
week of prayer, he pulls out each paper and prays, "Okay,
Lord, what are we going to do?"

What amazes Jim and me the most about this entire procedure is Jerry's attitude! His full counseling schedule means he hears about a lot of heartache, but it in no way affects his personality or his outlook on life. Whenever anyone encounters Jerry, they are greeted with an exuberant smile, a ton of energy, and the confident statement, "God is still on His throne!" Clearly, Jerry is secure and living out God's promises!

You and I can be just as secure—and joyful!—in God's promises as Jerry is. That's because of what we've been learning. We now know that God has a plan for us that is and will be good. And the assurance that He is still on His throne means that nothing can interfere with God's plans.

Jerry believes and lives out God's promise in Jeremiah 29:11. His example shows us how thinking of God's good plan for our lives as an adventure, a process, and an opportunity can improve our attitude toward life and its trials. Even in problem times, we can be positive in our faith in God's character and His promises.

God's Good Plan: Purging and Pruning

And here's another part of God's good plan: He is faithful to use life's difficulties to purge and prune us of all that does not contribute positively to the masterpiece He is creating. When my husband said, "Judy, this is a beautiful garden, but what happened over there?" he was pointing to an area that was not beautiful at all. He was pointing to the rocks that would have to be carted off, the rotten pieces of fencing that would have to be replaced, the dead tree that would have to be removed, the tree stump that would have to be ground into chips, the sick shrubs that would have to be dug out, and the packed earth that would have to be rototilled before it could sustain any plant life. Everything in that part of the yard was ugly, old, dead, diseased, and useless and would have to be eliminated and destroyed before Judy could complete her beautiful garden. That cleanup was part of her plan.

And God works the same way in our lives. Before His plan can come to full fruition in our lives, He must eliminate all that is old, dead, diseased, and useless in our character.

For instance, when we first meet Sarah in the Old Testament (her story is found in Genesis 11–23), she is impatient, contentious, angry, manipulative, and unbelieving. Her life with Abraham (her husband), Hagar (Abraham's concubine), and Ishmael (Abraham's son by Hagar) is characterized by tension and unfulfillment. But God worked in Sarah's life and used failures, consequences, time, and her unhappiness to bring her to a mature faith in Him. In fact, Sarah is listed in the New Testament (Hebrews 11) as an example of faith.

There's no doubt that a pruning process like Sarah underwent can be painful! But it gives us an opportunity to grow in faith as God works in our lives to eliminate the unattractive and the ineffective and bring about the beauty He has promised.

God's Good Nature

To better enjoy the security God provides, we must understand that He is trustworthy and His nature is good—100 percent good! We must firmly establish in our minds that God can only think and do good. Conversely, God cannot think or do evil. James warns, "Let no one say when he is tempted, 'I am tempted by God'; for *God cannot be tempted by evil, nor does He Himself tempt anyone*" (James 1:13). In fact, God cannot even look upon evil. The prophet Habakkuk declared, "You are of purer eyes than to behold evil, and *cannot look on wickedness*" (Habakkuk 1:13).

Knowing of God's goodness is vital because our thoughts influence our behavior. If, for instance, we believe God can think evil thoughts and do evil deeds, we will never be secure and confident in His love. No, we will suspect that evil and harm are around every corner! But if we regulate our thoughts by the truth that God cannot think or do evil—ever!—we can then proceed through each day of our lives living fully in the promise of God's love and His goodness.

Remembering God's goodness—To help keep my thoughts in line with the truth that God cannot think or do evil, I have a collection of "goodness verses." They guide my thoughts and my prayers whenever I need to remember that I am secure in God. Here are a few to help you start your own list.

> Every good gift and every perfect gift is from above, and comes down from the Father of lights, with whom there is no variation or shadow of turning (James 1:17).

> Oh, taste and see that the LORD is good (Psalm 34:8).

> Oh, that men would give thanks to the LORD for His goodness, and for His wonderful works to the children of men! For He satisfies the

longing soul, and fills the hungry soul with goodness (Psalm 107:8-9).

The LORD is good, a stronghold in the day of trouble; and He knows those who trust in Him (Nahum 1:7).

Verses like these have helped me as well as the women who have asked me for counsel. Gayle is one such woman. She came to me when the circumstances of her life gave her reason to wonder about God and His goodness. So I encouraged her to memorize one of these "goodness verses" each week. Memorizing these words of truth and hope gave her comfort, and I could refer her to them to remind her of God's goodness and her security in Him.

Praying about God's goodness—I also had Gayle write out a prayer using these verses. Then, every time she thought about her situation or had to face the people involved, she could remember her prayer and again remind herself of the truth about God. Whenever she felt anger, sadness, and discouragement, she could turn to her prayer and remember that God is good and that His plan for her is good. And you can do the same! Here's the prayer:

Father God, I want to thank You for Your sovereign power in my life, that You arrange all circumstances—past, present and future—for good for me because I love You and am called according to Your purposes (Romans 8:28). It gives me great assurance and security in You to know that You know the plans You have for me regarding (*situation, person, problem*) I also can rest in the fact that You want only the best for me, a future and a hope (Jeremiah 29:11). Help me to remember that Your provision is all encompassing.

Writing your own prayer and incorporating your selection of "goodness verses" in it will help you view the challenges and hurts of your life through Scripture's truth. As you draw closer to God in prayer and focus on His goodness, He will bless you with His peace and the assurance of His love.

Looking to the Reward

Have you ever planned a vacation to mark the end of a long project or a special evening out to celebrate the completion of a difficult task? Rewards are powerful motivators because we can endure hard times as long as we know there is something good at the end. We can work hard and sacrifice meals, sleep, and fun when the goal and the reward are worthwhile.

Because God knew that the 70-year exile would be difficult for His people, He gave the Israelites something to look forward to and promised them a "reward" in Jeremiah 29:11: There would be an expected end, a future and a hope, the restoration of peace and prosperity. God did not want "that unexpectant apathy which is the terrible accompaniment of so much worldly sorrow...to be an ingredient in the lot of the Jews."[1] The promise and the "reward" He held out offered them security, hope, and a reason to persevere.

Knowing of God's planned and future reward ministers to me (and you, too) in three different ways.

Rebuke—God's promise rebukes me when I am tempted to doubt Him and question His management of my life. I can almost hear God chiding, "Wait a minute! The plans I have for you are for good and not for evil, and I will indeed bring that good about. I *will* bring you to an expected end."

Although I don't know the specifics of this promised end, I can trust in the fact that He knows.

Comfort—God's promise gives me comfort. He uses Jeremiah 29:11 to calm my emotions. Through the prophet's words, God whispers, "It's okay. You don't have to worry or wonder about anything. I know the plans I have for you, and they are plans for good and not for evil. I'll bring you to the expected end."

God uses this verse to remind me that He has complete knowledge of my life, a plan for me that is for good, and the ability to make that plan happen. This assurance brings me great peace.

Encouragement—Jeremiah 29:11 also offers encouragement. Through the promise in this verse, God encourages me when I am tempted to despair. He prods, "Keep going! Don't give up your hope. And don't worry about the end. The plans I have for you are plans for good and not for evil, to bring you to an expected end."

Through this promise, God reminds me that, no matter how hard or long the journey, I am going to get to the end—where the reward is waiting. And the end is going to be good!

And I've saved the best for last! God's greatest promise for His children is heaven. Heaven is the expected end for all who name Jesus as Lord and Savior. Ultimately, the final future and hope for us who are God's children is heaven, where there will be fullness of joy and pleasures forevermore at His right hand (Psalm 16:11).

Loving God…Even More

*W*here does life find you today? What difficult times are you enduring? What situation seems to be unbearable? Well, you can be encouraged because God's powerful promise leaves no phase or issue of life uncovered! Jeremiah 29:11 assures us that God's plans, for us personally and for His people in general, are for good, not evil. In God and His sure Word, we find security for any and every situation we'll encounter in life—birth, death, marriage, singleness, widowhood, poverty, persecution, suffering the unknown of a move, or the permanence of being in an unpleasant place.

One morning a pastor's wife called to tell me that her husband was resigning from his church. Margo reported, "Elizabeth, I've been reciting Jeremiah 29:11 all day long! I know God was involved in bringing us here. I know we have learned many lessons and been used in many ways. I also know God has a plan for us and that it's good. He knows where we are going!" In the midst of all that she was feeling due to her life being turned upside down, Margo was using her mind to love God, to reach out to Him, to focus on the truths of Scripture, and to live out God's promise. Margo was dealing with fear, disappointment, worry, anger, confusion, and hurt as she anticipated saying goodbye, being uprooted from her home, and moving in an unknown direction to an unknown place.

Oh, but she is confident in God's perfect plan! And you and I can be, too! The foundations of our daily lives may suddenly collapse, and the security of our income may slip away, but we know about God, His goodness, and His promises. Therefore we can enjoy victory in our thought lives. We can love God with all our minds as we bring each thought into captivity to the truth of Jeremiah 29:11.

Accepting the Unacceptable

❦⸻❦

*Oh, the depth of the riches
both of the wisdom and knowledge of God!
How unsearchable are His judgments and
His ways past finding out!*

ROMANS 11:33

$\mathcal{R}$ESPONDING TO
LIFE'S TURNING POINTS

⟳∞⟲

Oh, the depth of the riches
both of the wisdom and knowledge of God!
How unsearchable are His judgments
and His ways past finding out!

ROMANS 11:33 NASB

$\mathcal{T}$HE SUN ROSE THAT MORNING JUST as it had risen every day of her life. As she ran through her list of chores, there was no hint that today her life would be transformed from the mundane to the mysterious. But something happened that day which changed everything—forever. Seconds after it happened, gone were her hopes of the quiet life she had imagined for herself. Gone were the comfort and safety of a predictable routine. Gone was the peaceful existence she and her family had known, the existence that had led her to expect a simple and unremarkable future.

These words describe a singular day in the life of Mary, the mother of Jesus. The scriptural account for that day simply says, "And having come in, the angel said to her..."

(Luke 1:28). "The angel" was Gabriel, sent from God. And what he said to her sent her world reeling. It completely changed her life. Nothing would ever be the same because she had been chosen to be the mother of God's Son. She would bring into the world its Savior, Lord, and King. Nothing could ever be the same for Mary!

Turning Points

Perhaps you can point to a day in your life that changed everything for you, a day after which nothing would ever be the same—a day when dark clouds hid the sun. Such turning points in life can shake us to the core. Such turning points can also send us to God, His Word, and His promises.

Did the pivotal day in your life begin normally? Often our routine is well underway, and nothing out of the ordinary is happening—until the phone rings, the letter arrives, or the appointment unfolds. Whatever the event was for you, it signified a totally changed life. Calling such an event "the turning point," Corrie ten Boom wrote, "The turning point may be announced by the ring of a telephone or a knock on the door."[1] In her own life, "the turning point" was a knock on her door by German soldiers. Her life turned from normal to horrendous as she entered a Nazi concentration camp.

What are we to do at such turning points in life? How can we handle the changes after a life-altering incident and the new kind of life that follows? And what are we to think about the unexplainable and unexpected things that happen to us? How can we accept these mysterious events that clearly spell out God's will for us? How can we accept what seems to be unacceptable?

Accepting God's Will

We can learn from Mary some answers to these questions. The gospel of Luke shows us how, at this major turning point in her life, Mary humbly accepted the news from Gabriel that she would bear God's Son. Mary is noted as a woman of very few words, but this announcement from Gabriel caused her to carefully and thoughtfully pose one question—How? "How can this be, since I am a virgin?" (Luke 1:34 NASB).

Mary's question—a perfectly natural one since she was unmarried and a virgin—received an answer that lay in the supernatural realm: "The Holy Spirit will come upon you, and the power of the Highest will overshadow you; therefore, also, that Holy One who is to be born will be called the Son of God" (verse 35). In other words, the conception would be a miracle! And that was all the explanation Mary got!

Unable to understand what would happen to her, Mary nevertheless consented to God's will for her life. She boldly declared, "Behold the maidservant of the Lord! Let it be to me according to your word" (verse 38).

This simple scenario allows us a glimpse into God's "ways," which Romans 11:33 describes as "past finding out" (NKJV) or "unfathomable" (NASB). Here was a girl, probably a young teenager, going about the daily business of growing up, and one day, by one judgment from God, everything changed. Not only her life, but the entire world changed...forever. God acted and God spoke...and things would never be the same.

When God spoke to Mary through Gabriel and told her that she had been chosen to be the mother of Jesus, her life changed completely. For Mary, God's revealed will meant being pregnant before she was married and being branded a fornicator. God's will meant trouble with her husband-to-be, trouble at home, trouble in Nazareth, and trouble among her children. God's will meant a life of tension as Mary and her baby were hunted down, as she fled from country to country, and as her remarkable Son caused violent reactions in the hearts of the people He met. And for Mary, God's will meant a soul pierced with sorrow (Luke 2:35) as she followed her Son on His path of pain to the cross (John 19:25-27).

Yet when the angel appeared, Mary accepted the news of God's will for her life with the statement, "Let it be to me according to your word."

The Mentality of a Handmaiden

How was Mary able to accept Gabriel's startling announcement? Why was she able to accept this radical turning point in her life?

Clue #1 is found in Mary's reference to herself as "the maidservant of the Lord" or "the handmaid of the Lord" (Luke 1:38 KJV). In the New Testament, a "handmaid" is the same as a bondservant, "whose will was not his own but who rather was committed to another. The slave was obligated to perform his master's will without question or delay."[2] A handmaiden would sit silently and watch for hand signals from her mistress (Psalm 123:2). Through these motions rather than any spoken command, the mistress would communicate her wishes. Her handmaiden, having been trained to watch for these signs, would then obey them—without question or hesitation.[3]

As this cultural background suggests, it is significant that Mary chose to describe herself as a "handmaid." Clearly, she had cultivated the attitude and the mentality of a hand-maiden in her fine-tuned attentiveness to her God. She no longer viewed herself as her own or considered herself to have rights. Instead, she was wholly committed to God. Her one purpose in life was to obey her Master's will… quickly, quietly, and without question.

So, that day in Nazareth when God moved His hand and signaled His will, Mary, His devoted handmaiden, noticed. At the flick of God's finger, she responded, "Behold the maidservant of the Lord!" Whatever God wanted, this humble maidservant was willing to do, even though it meant that everything in her life changed—forever. Mary saw herself as God's handmaiden and so accepted His will for her life.

A Knowledge of God

Clue #2 explains why Mary was able to accept Gabriel's startling announcement of God's will for her life. It also explains her ability to accept this radical turning point in her life: Mary had a working knowledge of God. She knew God well enough to trust Him and His love for her. And this knowledge helped her accept His will.

Hear Mary's heart and her words of praise in Luke 1:46-55, the song known as the Magnificat. Her outpouring begins with "my soul magnifies the Lord" (verse 46). And her inspired words of exaltation continue on for nine verses, containing 15 quotations from the Old Testament.[4] Clearly, Mary had "majored on the majors"! She knew about God and His mercy, about His provision and His faithfulness to her forefathers.

As one author has observed, the number of scriptures quoted in the Magnificat show that "Mary knew God, through the books of Moses and the Psalms and the writings of the prophets. She had a deep reverence for the Lord God in her heart because she knew what He had done in the history of her people."⁵ Mary knew God well. And knowing God and recognizing His infinite wisdom and knowledge enables us, like Mary, to accept what He has ordained for our lives.

And not only can we accept what God has planned for us, but we can also rejoice, knowing that His plans for us are for good. We can actually look forward with joy to the life and riches God has in store for us!

The Depth of the Riches of God

As we end this chapter, I want us to notice the powerful truths about God that are revealed in Romans 11:33. Four facts about God and His ways are on display in this one verse of Scripture. We'll look more closely at each "fact" in the next few chapters, but here are a few bits of information that make them more understandable.

Learning about the background—In chapters 1–11 of the book of Romans, the apostle Paul pours forth the central truths of Christianity and conveys the great doctrines of grace. And in chapter 11, he deals with many lofty topics like God's righteousness and mercy, the mystery of salvation, and justification by faith. Finally, in verses 33-36 Paul can bear it no longer and bursts into worshipful praise. Standing at the heights of Christianity, he exults over what he sees, and realizes all he does not see:

> Oh, the depth of the riches both of the wisdom
> and knowledge of God! How unsearchable are
> His judgments and His ways past finding out!

"For who has known the mind of the LORD? Or who has become His counselor? Or who has first given to Him and it shall be repaid to him?" For of Him and through Him and to Him are all things, to whom be glory forever. Amen (Romans 11:33-36).

Learning about the language—Look again at the words "depth...unsearchable...past finding out." As I studied various books on Romans to more fully understand Romans 11:33, I had to ask my husband a question. I was using quite a few of his books, and many of them had Greek words scattered throughout them. Now, I don't know Greek, but I could tell there were a number of repeated Greek characters surrounding the nouns *wisdom, knowledge, judgments,* and *ways.* So I took the reference books to Jim, who does know Greek, and he explained the Greek letters in today's vernacular. He said that whenever I saw this particular Greek letter formation, I should think of and add the word "not."

That would make Paul's words read something like this: "Can you trace God's wisdom (...or knowledge...or judgments...or ways)? *Not!* Can you find it? *Not!* Does it have footprints to follow? *Not!* Are there tracks? *Not!* Can you go to the depths of it? *Not!* Can it be exhausted? *Not!* Is there an end to it? *Not!*" In other words, because God's wisdom, knowledge, judgments, and ways lie in the realm of God, can we understand them? *Not!* Therefore the translators of different Bible translations describe the four elements concerning God's manner as un-understandable, unsearchable, inscrutable, inexhaustible, unfathomable, and impossible to grasp. Why? Again, because they lie in the realm of God.

I have to tell you that I experienced something of a breakthrough in understanding...when I realized there would be a myriad of events in life that I would never understand. God works in mysterious ways, which means they are ways that cannot be explained. In the chapters that follow, we'll look more in-depth at the four facts about God that can help us to better accept the unacceptable, to better understand the un-understandable! Such knowledge, along with cultivating the mentality of a bondservant or handmaiden in our relationship with God, can help us to respond to the turning points in life in the way that Mary did—"Behold the maidservant of the Lord! Let it be to me according to your word" (Luke 1:38).

Loving God...Even More

*W*hen it comes to loving God with all our mind, we do a better job of it when we, like Mary, pay attention to nurturing the mentality of a servant or a handmaiden. That means praying and desiring and purposing to serve God as He calls us, when He calls us, and where He calls us.

When we can respond to whatever is happening in our lives with Mary's heart-attitude toward God expressed in words like these—"I am the Lord's slave. Let it be as you say"⁶—then we can know that we are loving God with all our mind. We can also, by His grace, consent to God's will and to the unsearchable judgments of our infinitely good and merciful God, even without comprehension.

26

MAJORING ON
THE MINORS

⤫

*Oh, the depth of the riches
both of the wisdom
and knowledge of God!*

ROMANS 11:33

I'VE BEEN EXTREMELY BLESSED TO know some incredible Christian women who have modeled faith in God and service to Him. One of these very special women is my Sarah. I first met this amazing woman 25 years ago. She inspires everyone she meets...and I was no exception! Her wisdom, her love for God, and her commitment to memorizing Scripture helped shape my ministry and message.

I vividly remember, for instance, asking her a question: "Sarah, if you were to write a book for women, what would it be about?" Her answer changed my life! She said, "Elizabeth, I don't like many of the books I see when I go into Christian bookstores. There are so few books for women about God. If I were to write a book to share with women what I have learned through the years, I would call it *Forever Father*. Women today have so many problems simply because they don't know God. We are majoring on the minors."

Focusing on God

"Majoring on the minors"—I have literally spent hours thinking about these words! And Sarah's observation and her statement made to me those decades ago changed my philosophy of ministry, my studies, the books I choose to read, the way I use my time, and the ideas I share with others when I teach and write. Her observation also explained to me why she is such a powerful model of faith. Throughout her life, Sarah has majored on knowing God. As a result, she possesses clear vision, a sound mind, and the wisdom to know what really counts in the Christian life.

And what really counts in the Christian life is knowing God. Why? Because that knowledge is foundational if we are to truly love Him, live for Him, and joyfully serve Him. It is, however, much easier to major on the minors than on the person of God. For instance, we tend to center our attention on our problems...rather than on the Person of our all-loving and all-powerful God. We tend to focus on our troubles...and forget to trust our faithful Lord. We tend to look down at the entangling evils of the world around us...and fail to look up at God's heavenly majesty.

And, sadly, efforts today in our churches tend to major on meeting needs, providing support, and facilitating fellowship. Yet many people seem to have more needs than ever, and the old needs are still unmet. We wonder why we have problems we can't handle. What we really need is to know God, have better knowledge of God, and have more knowledge of God...instead of majoring on the minors.

We, as individuals and in the church, need to be con-
sciously majoring on "the majors," on strengthening ourselves and others in the major areas of Christianity. What
are some of "the majors"? God's attributes, the life of Christ,
men and women of the Bible, books of the Bible, and our
New Testament position in Christ. Emphasis also needs to
be placed on the spiritual life, faith, wisdom, prayer, and
the Scriptures. As A.W. Tozer writes in his classic book *The
Knowledge of the Holy,*

> A right conception of God is basic not only to
> systematic theology but to practical Christian
> living as well....I believe there is scarcely an
> error in doctrine or a failure in applying Christian
> ethics that cannot be traced finally to imperfect
> and ignoble thoughts about God.[1]

A.W. Tozer—and my Sarah—calls us to know God, to
focus on Him—to major on the majors! And Romans 11:33
is a "major" that teaches us four facts about God.

Acknowledging the Wisdom of God

> *Oh, the depth of the riches
> ...of the wisdom...of God!*

Where do you get wisdom? If you're like me, you go
primarily to the Bible. I try to read from Proverbs each day,
and I often follow along in a commentary. Studying the
lives of men and women in the Old and New Testament
and reading the words of believers who have gone before
me also teaches me wisdom.

Then there are Christian mentors and teachers. Through
the years these wise people have been great sources of

wisdom. Also, I never hesitate to follow the example of Queen Esther. This wise woman never made a significant decision without first asking for counsel. Whenever I have asked for advice from my husband, pastor, peers, friends, and teachers, I've been blessed and guided by God's wisdom.

God, however, doesn't have to study the Bible or read a book. Neither does He need to seek counsel or advice from others. No, God Himself *is* wisdom! And He derives it from no other source. And don't forget how we described the four facts about God found in Romans 11:33, including His wisdom—it is unsearchable, inscrutable, inexhaustible, and unfathomable. It is impossible to understand. Therefore, God's wisdom calls us to faith.

Heeding God's Wisdom as a Parent

Soon after I became a Christian, I had an important decision to make—whether to choose the world's wisdom or God's wisdom when it came to training my children. Previously I had decided that as a parent, I would not physically discipline my children. Instead I would reward, reason with, and convince them to do things my way. But in my daily reading of Proverbs, I was hearing God's instruction to discipline my two preschool daughters. I was also realizing that such discipline might involve the correction of a spanking from time to time. The world was telling me one thing, and God's Word was clearly telling me the opposite. Knowing what God said, I knew I had to obey, so I purchased a little six-inch wooden spoon...just in case!

Sure enough, the day came when I got an opportunity to do things God's way. When my young darlings acted up in a big way and needed to be disciplined, I went into my bedroom and prayed, then picked up the little spoon, explained why I needed to do what I was about to do, and spanked them each with one little pop (which was more like one little pat!).

It couldn't have even hurt, but probably due to shock, both of my girls began to cry. And a "miracle" occurred in our kitchen that day as each little girl hugged one of my legs and cried in unison, "Oh, Mommy, I won't ever do that again!"

Yes, my children cried—and I cried with them—on those rare occasions when I had to use that tiny wooden spoon. But suddenly my girls started following my instructions and listening when I spoke. We began to have a home of peace instead of chaos. As Jim and I offered behavioral guidelines and biblical discipline for our girls, we learned the wisdom of obeying the wisdom of God.

This seemingly small step was major for me because I was doing what I understood God to be telling me through His Word. But I was doing it by faith...because I didn't understand God's wisdom, how it would work, or why it would help. I was, by faith, applying God's wisdom to my life. Without completely understanding how to apply His wise directive to discipline my children, I believed, I trusted, and I obeyed as best I could. As I said, God's unsearchable, inscrutable, inexhaustible, unfathomable, and impossible-to-understand wisdom calls us to faith! On the other side of faith and obedience come the dawning of understanding and some very positive results.

Acknowledging the Knowledge of God

Oh, the depth of the riches
...of the...knowledge...of God!

Closely related to honoring God's wisdom is appreciating His knowledge. And I ask you again, where do you go to get knowledge? If you're like me, you read books, take classes, and watch educational television. We can earn degrees, obtain licenses, and enroll in continuing education courses. We can investigate the various branches of mathematics, physics, chemistry, biology, and the other sciences. We can plumb the mysteries of DNA and genetics and reach beyond the atmosphere to the moon and distant planets. And we can use computers to manage the increasing amount of knowledge available to us in this era of information explosion.

God, however, doesn't need books, computers, encyclopedias, teachers, or classes. No, God Himself is the source of all knowledge! As the Author of all things, God knows all that can be known. And like His wisdom, His knowledge is unsearchable, inscrutable, unfathomable, inexhaustible, and unexplainable. It is impossible to understand. We cannot begin to define God's knowledge. We know, simply and profoundly, that nothing is hidden from Him or incomprehensible to Him.

And what is it that God knows?

Realizing God Knows All About Us

Among all that God knows is His knowledge of your particular situation—and mine, too. God knows our joys and sorrows. He knows our strengths and weaknesses. If we are married, He also knows our spouses' strengths and weaknesses. If we have children, God knows about each one of them—their temperaments, their needs, and the challenges we face raising them.

If there are no children, God knows that, too, and He knows His purpose in it, as well as our suffering if we desire children. And if we don't have a marriage partner and aren't blessed with the gift of singleness, God knows it, and He knows our pain and how He plans to use our lives for Him. God also knows our finances and our jobs, our problems with our neighbors and our in-laws, our desires to serve Him, and the questions in our hearts.

And, of course, God knows our problems. The difficulties we face are no secret to Him. In fact, He has known about them forever. The challenges we face are known to Him. In fact, He knows—and has known since the beginning of time—exactly how He would use them to draw us closer to Him and to make us more like Christ. God's knowledge extends throughout time and includes our past, our present, and our future.

Knowing that God knows all about the things I've listed—and more!—certainly makes it easier for me to accept whatever comes my way. The fact of God's knowledge also helps me feel His presence with me, especially when life is difficult.

Put simply, God knows all about you and all about me. He knows our hurts, our wants, and our needs. Therefore, He understands us and we are always understood. We can know that He knows all about us and cares deeply about our feelings, our ideas, and our concerns. We can never say to God, "But You don't understand." We can be confident that even when no one else knows or understands, He does!

Loving God...Even More

Knowing more about God's wisdom and knowledge (which we will never fully know and understand!) has caused me to think of them as two bookends. When our family experienced the near-destruction of our home in a killer earthquake while living in Southern California, the violent shaking emptied all of our books off the library shelves. As I stood surveying that room full of rubble, weeping over the ruin of our home, I prayed to God about what I could do to bring even some tiny bit of order to the chaos I was looking at.

It was then I spotted one of our bookends. I picked it up and searched through the books and the debris until I found its mate. Then I placed the matching set of bookends on a shelf and began putting books—any books— between them. By finding the different sets of bookends and placing books between them I did finally bring order to chaos.

And my friend, that's the way it is in your life when you love God and count on His love, when you trust in His wisdom and count on His knowledge. Simply take all of the un-understandable events in your life—the wonder-ings, the why's, and the bewilderment over the things that happen to you and to others—and file them between God's wisdom and God's knowledge. You don't under-stand these occurrences...and you never will...because you can't! But God does. And so we rest in Him. Peace and order—and greater love for God—is yours when you place the impossible-to-understand issues and incidents in your life between His infinite wisdom and His all-encompassing knowledge. Oh, the depth of the riches both of the wisdom and knowledge of God!

27

*T*RUSTING GOD
IN THE DARK

❦

How unsearchable are His judgments
and His ways past finding out!

ROMANS 11:33

*I*S THERE ANYTHING IN YOUR LIFE you struggle to understand? Do you ever wonder why certain things are the way they are? Do you hear yourself questioning something that has or hasn't happened in your life? As we are learning in our walk through Romans 11:33, we must make a conscious effort to accept God's wisdom and knowledge and then live accordingly.

In years gone by, I learned much about God and His wisdom from a young mother who carried a baby full-term knowing for most of the pregnancy that the child would live only a few brief hours due to a genetic defect. I praise God for the triumphant five-page letter this grieving mom wrote to me listing the multitude of lessons God taught her as those months crawled by. She has learned, as hard as it was, to accept God's wisdom in His choice of this purpose for her. She learned to trust Him in the dark. She came to trust in God's knowledge of the situation and of the *whys* of her situation.

As hard as it is and in whatever the situation (everything from disciplining a child to having your baby die in your arms), we must acknowledge, as Paul did, "Oh, the depth of the riches both of the wisdom and knowledge of God!" When we don't understand, like, or agree with the way life has gone, we are to bow before God and once again confess that we cannot understand His wisdom and knowledge. In faith, we are to accept His wisdom, His Word, and His workings, and trust in Him...even in the dark.

Remembering God's Wisdom and Knowledge

For a moment think about what we've been learning about God from Romans 11:33. Think back on my wise Sarah's comment that we have so many problems simply because we don't know God. We've been getting to know God better in the chapters in this section by considering His love, His wisdom, and His knowledge. So I pray that by now your problems look differently when laid before the infinite wisdom and knowledge of your loving God. After all, how big are your problems next to an omnipotent, all-powerful God?

As I suggested in the previous chapter, think of God's wisdom and knowledge as the bookends for your life, holding up all of its incomprehensible happenings and offering a sense of order to God's mysterious working. After all, nothing is ever unknown, nothing is ever overlooked, and nothing is ever a surprise to God. And, as A.W. Tozer reminds us, in all that ever happens to you and me, God in His wisdom is always working toward predestined goals with His flawless precision.[1]

By God's grace, you and I can better accept every event in our lives when we realize that *all* of the details and elements of our lives are in the hands of our infinitely wise God who knows us and loves us as no one else does. This perfect wisdom calls us to faith. Again, Tozer writes, "The testimony of faith is that, no matter how things look in this fallen world, all God's acts are wrought in perfect wisdom."[2]

Although God's ways are often mysterious, by faith we believe in the infinite and holy wisdom behind them. By faith we trust in the wisdom of God that stands behind the events we don't understand. As Oswald Chambers points out, "Trustfulness is based on confidence in God whose ways I do not understand; if I did, there would be no need for trust."[3]

Acknowledging God's Judgments

Hear again the heart of Paul in Romans 11:33. Besides praising God for His wisdom and His knowledge, Paul also praises God for His judgments and His ways. To begin, he exclaims, "How unsearchable are His *judgments*...!" God's judgments have to do with God's decisions and His "rules" and decrees. His judgments reveal His plans for the universe, for the human race, and for you and me individually.

For instance, as parents we make the rule, "Don't play in the street." Does the child fully understand the reasons behind that decree or judgment? No. Does the child need to understand? No. The child simply needs to accept the parents' rule and obey it.

And we, as God's children, need to do the same. It's not necessary for us to understand God's rules, decrees, or judgments. Furthermore, we aren't expected to always understand them. In fact, like God's wisdom and knowledge, we can't understand all of God's judgments...because they are un-understandable, unsearchable, inscrutable, inexhaustible, unfathomable, and impossible to grasp.

However, it is necessary that we accept those judgments and the events in our lives that result from them...even when we don't understand the reasons behind them. Put simply, our duty is like that of a child—to accept the rules and obey. We don't need to understand why things are the way they are. We only need to follow the rules.

Here's another thought: We can either argue with God or accept His judgments. The choice is ours. And the choice of attitude is ours, too. We can rant and rave, struggle and search, seek revenge and hold grudges, become bitter or bewildered...or we can accept what is happening in our lives as part of God's judgments.

Accepting Without Answers

And that's what the young Mary did. She certainly couldn't understand Gabriel's announcement of God's judgment that she would be the mother of the Messiah. (No one, apart from God, ever has!) She also couldn't understand completely how she would conceive the child. (And no one has ever understood this either!) After all, this plan came from the mind of God.

So Mary had a choice to make. She could either argue with and question God's action...or she could accept His judgment in her life. Either way, the outcome would be the same: She would give birth to the Son of God. She had a choice, however, about her attitude and her conduct. She chose to accept this unsearchable judgment of God even though she didn't understand it. She consented to God's judgment without comprehending the how, the why, or the effects it would have on her life. She asked, "How?" but accepted God's will without receiving any answers. She consented without comprehension, saying, "Behold the maidservant of the Lord! Let it be to me according to your word" (Luke 1:38).

Like Mary, you and must remember that the events in our lives are the results of God's judgments. We must accept in faith that the events of our lives are accomplishing something in God's plan for us and for His world. He is at work and in control of our universe and our lives, and He has His reasons...which are un-understandable, unsearchable, inscrutable, inexhaustible, unfathomable, and impossible to grasp. The reasons behind His decisions remain in the realm of God, and you and I must rest in the knowledge that they are His domain, not ours. Therefore, we probably won't understand the how's and the why's on this side of heaven.

Acknowledging God's Ways

"How unsearchable are His judgments," Paul exults, "and His *ways* past finding out!" What are God's ways? To begin our understanding, God's ways are the methods by which He carries out His judgments.[4] We must quickly and humbly admit that God's ways—the roads or paths He takes to carry out His judgments and fulfill His purposes— are not usually the way we would do things!

No, we cannot comprehend God's ways. As Paul tells us, they are "past finding out!" The very fact that they are God's ways points to His independence from all human beings and reminds us of the vast difference between Him, the Creator, and us, the created.[5] It is only reasonable, then, that we find God's ways (like His wisdom, knowledge, and judgments) to be un-understandable, unsearchable, inscrutable, inexhaustible, unfathomable, and impossible to grasp—past finding out!

You see, God is in His own unfathomable category. He is not like us and cannot be understood. The prophet Isaiah revealed this truth centuries ago when, speaking on God's behalf, he wrote, "For My thoughts are not your thoughts, nor are your ways My ways….For as the heavens are higher than the earth, so are My ways higher than your ways, and My thoughts than your thoughts" (Isaiah 55:8-9). Speaking on behalf of God, the psalmist offered this rebuke—"You thought that I was altogether like you" (Psalm 50:21).

Paul's rhetorical question in Romans 11:34 further underscores the mystery of God's ways—"For who has known the mind of the LORD?" The only answer is, "No one." As the Living Bible says simply, "How impossible it is for us to understand his decisions and his methods!" (verse 33).

Great freedom and peace is ours when we acknowledge that God is infinitely superior to us in His wisdom, knowledge, judgments, and ways, and when we accept—without understanding—His work in the world and in our lives.

Dear friend, are you beginning to understand why this chapter is entitled "Trusting God in the Dark"? It's because (and I cannot say it enough!) God's judgments and ways, like His wisdom and knowledge, are un-understandable, unsearchable, inscrutable, inexhaustible, unfathomable, and impossible to grasp—past finding out!

So what can we do? We must trust God in the dark! We must trust Him without understanding. Like the psalmist advised in Psalm 46:10, we must simply "be still, and know that I am God." We must "cease striving" (NASB) and, in essence, know that "it is I, God, who is doing this!"

Loving God...Even More

Un-understandable, unsearchable, inscrutable, inexhaustible, unfathomable, and impossible to grasp—past finding out! This God is our God...forever and ever! We will never fully know God or fully recognize or appreciate His deep love for us. But hopefully you are beginning to understand more about Him. And with that understanding, you are more willing to freely yield yourself to His plans, His wisdom, His knowledge, His judgments, and His ways— for you and your life.

Although in your pain you may sometimes ask "Why?" you can fully trust that God loves you and that His plan for you is good. In your deeper understanding, you will also not resist His work in your life. Instead you will know that He closes and opens doors for your good. You will realize that He uses the fires of life to purify your faith, to shape you into Christ's image, and to cause you to love Him...even more.

28

$\mathscr{A}$CCEPTING
THE UNACCEPTABLE

$\sim\!\!\!\!\!\!\infty\!\!\!\!\!\sim$

Oh, the depth of the riches
both of the wisdom and knowledge of God!
How unsearchable are His judgments and
His ways past finding out!

ROMANS 11:33

$\mathscr{A}$CKNOWLEDGING THE TRUTH that God's judgments are unsearchable and His ways mysterious is not merely a theological exercise. Acknowledging that God's ways are not our ways and accepting that truth has made a real difference in my life, and it can in yours, too.

Here's what happened...

A Problem

There was a period of time in my life when I experienced "one of those situations" that had me wondering what God was doing in my life. A woman in authority over me seemed to delight in holding me back from growing in the Lord and in keeping me from stretching my wings as I sought to serve Him.

During the eight long years of this painful relationship, I kept asking, "Can't anyone see what is happening here? Don't You see, God? Just look my way! It's so obvious that she's tripping me up as I try to serve You! How can You let this go on time after time?"

Every day for eight years—day after dreary day, year after frustrating year—I spoke daily to God and my husband about this seemingly hopeless and pointless situation. I couldn't stop thinking about it...and I didn't know what to do. My preoccupation seriously affected my spiritual life. For instance, whenever I sat down to have my devotions or whenever I attended a worship service, I found myself thinking about my problem and this problem person! For eight years I limped along in my spiritual growth.

A Scripture

I finally experienced a turning point. The morning began like any other morning. Jim was at work, our girls had been dropped off at school, and I was going through my usual daily routine. When it was time for my morning walk, I grabbed the pack of memory verses I wanted to review and headed out the door.

This particular pack of verses happened to be the first one I had ever memorized. I had been reviewing its 72 verses regularly through the years. But this time, when I came to verse #72—the final verse on my walk—I heard Romans 11:33 differently.

> Oh, the depth of the riches both of the wisdom
> and knowledge of God! How unsearchable are
> His judgments and His ways past finding out!

I said this by-now-familiar-scripture to myself as I neared home after my walk through my neighborhood, finally reaching the last sentence. And this time—after many years of knowing this verse—there was a break-through in my spirit as God used His Word to get through to my heart in a new way. The message of Romans 11:33 cleansed me! It washed over me! And it washed through me! Many of the unsearchable wonders of this verse opened up for me and gave me freedom from my long struggle with this particular woman.

What happened? Why did that familiar scripture suddenly come alive to me? All I know is that as I said the verse to myself, I found myself emphasizing the facts of...

God's wisdom,
God's knowledge,
His judgments, and
His ways.

There was no "me" in this verse. No, there was only God! And the fact that His wisdom, knowledge, judgments, and ways are unsearchable and "past finding out" was made personal to me. I saw that day that this truth spoke directly to my situation...and suddenly everything was okay.

What joy! What release! I remember stopping right on the sidewalk and saying aloud, "God did this! He allowed this, He planned this, He brought this. He knows this, and He has used it for my good. My situation is a part of His wisdom, His knowledge, His judgments, His ways—and those are past finding out!"

Freedom came as I realized right there on the sidewalk of a residential street in the San Fernando Valley that I didn't have to know or understand what was going on.

And it was okay to not understand! Furthermore, the situation—which was and always had been in the hands of my loving heavenly Father—would be okay.

An Instrument

God had definitely used Romans 11:33 in my life in other ways before that special morning. But when He spoke to me about the ongoing situation that had been such a burden for so long, I was so glad I had memorized this verse! You see, God's holy Word is an instrument He uses to guide, comfort, correct, rebuke, and teach us.

Dear friend, the passages we commit to memory are like a surgeon's sterilized tools—carefully arranged on instrument trays and ready for his expert use. When there's a problem in our life, God can pick up exactly the verse we need and cut right to our heart. He did so for me during that morning walk, and the surgery He performed on me with His Word set me free.

Now, meet another wonderful woman who taught me about the importance of memorizing Scripture. Each fall while Jim was a student at Talbot Theological Seminary, I drove for an hour in five o'clock freeway traffic to attend the opening session of the wives' fellowship. At those sessions, Dr. Carol Talbot told stunning stories of how God enabled her to serve Him as a missionary, a prisoner of war, and the wife of Louis Talbot.

One fall Mrs. Talbot talked about the impetigo she suffered from when she was a missionary in India. She shared how she underwent nine surgeries during the 17 years she battled this disease, and that battle was almost enough to cause her to give up her missions effort. But there was one thing that kept her from packing her bags and returning home. Every time she wanted to quit, God would bring to her mind a verse she had memorized. She would dismiss it—only to have another one rush in to take its place. She would dismiss that one, too. But again, God would send another one, and another, and another. Because she had memorized too many verses, she said, she was unable to give up her missionary service. In her final analysis, she shared, "God was using my disease to turn me from a pygmy into a giant."

Memorized Scripture can indeed turn us pygmies-in-the-faith into giants! When we love God with our mind and commit His Word to memory, He uses those pieces of Scripture as instruments for our growth in Him. When we store His Word in our mind, God draws from what we know and uses just the truth we need...at just the time we need it...and in just the way we need it!

That, my friend, is what happened to me that morning as I walked and routinely reviewed and recited just one of God's sharp instruments—Romans 11:33.

An Acceptance

But the use of this powerful scripture was in no way done! Through the years, God has used the lessons that Romans 11:33 teaches about Him to help me live out each day for Him with an acceptance of His dealings in my life. This single verse has taught me how to accept the unacceptable. The following principles, drawn from the application of this single verse, give me a lens through which to look at everything that happens to me. I offer them to you as well.

1. *I don't have to understand everything*—What freedom this acceptance brings! Imagine, no more

digging or dogged determination to get to the bottom of an issue.

2. *I don't need to understand everything*—What release this attitude brings! Why? Because it's an attitude that acknowledges that God is in control.

3. *I can't understand everything*—I am finite and limited, but God—who knows all and understands all—is infinite and limitless.

4. *Why ask "Why?"*—The man Job in the Old Testament never asked why when he was suffering. He worshiped instead. Notice very carefully what carried Job through his ordeal. Unlike the stance of the stoic (grin and bear it...or at least, grit your teeth and endure it), Job grabbed on to facts about God. Facts like—God is...

   ...too kind to do anything cruel,

   ...too wise to make a mistake,

   ...too deep to explain Himself.

   Believing these facts about God should erase all why's. We are to stop asking *Why?* and start looking at *Who* stands behind the scene. It is God in His absolute sovereignty! This calls us to worship.

5. *It's O.K.*—When we can say this to God about our unexplainable and seemingly unacceptable situations, we experience the rest of faith and the peace of faith.

6. *Let it go*—Pry your grip off your problem, and let it be gone forever. Oh, the freedom you will experience, even without any change, when you accept the unacceptable.

7. *Let God be God*—And what is He? Un-understandable, unsearchable, inscrutable, inexhaustible, unfathomable, and impossible to grasp.

8. *Let go of your right to know*—Stop demanding answers from God. Cease saying to God, "I'm not getting up from prayer until You tell me or show me why this is happening!"

9. *These are God's judgments*—Whatever has happened to you, it is a part of *God's* judgments... and they are "unsearchable." You will never understand or know why, so you must accept the unacceptable.

10. *These are God's ways*—Again, note the emphasis on *God*. Whatever has happened to you, it has to do with *His* ways, and they are "past finding out!" Again, you will never understand or find out, so you must accept the unacceptable.

11. *No vengeance!*—(And please note, that's spelled n-o, not k-n-o-w!) God is the Author and Creator of your situation. He has a plan and a blueprint for your life that includes your situation and any people involved. God says to you, "Never take your own revenge, beloved, but leave room for the wrath of God, for it is written, 'VENGEANCE, IS MINE, I WILL REPAY, says the Lord" (Romans 12:19).

12. *It's not them, it's Him!*—One person does not have the power to limit, alter, or change your life. People are only God's instruments, and He uses them to conform you to the image of His dear Son.

For eight years, I wasted time and emotional energy on a situation that was causing me real distress. But it was a situation God knew all about—and had allowed. Those years were rocky and miserable because I didn't understand that the problem was evidence of God's unsearchable wisdom and knowledge, evidence of His unfathomable judgments and ways.

And today? I still don't understand the reasons why my ongoing problem occurred. But guess what? It no longer matters! You see, now I am free! I can accept that God's ways aren't my ways, and I don't need to understand.

And there's more! Finally, because of all God has taught me through Romans 11:33, I am also determined never to waste my time or emotional energy like that again (and, praise Him, I don't think I have!). Instead, I am intent on remembering that God's judgments and ways are not like mine. I want to defer to His wisdom and knowledge. I want to say, along with Mary, "Behold the maidservant of the Lord! Let it be to me according to your word" (Luke 1:38). I want to accept the unacceptable.

Loving God . . . Even More

*W*hat greater way is there to show our love for God than to fully accept His will and His ways in our lives? Than to trust Him fully and completely...even in the dark? Than to accept the unacceptable? And I think you'll agree that this ability to accept His hand in our lives comes more easily when we seek to love Him with all our mind.

It is my prayer that you will want to give God's Word a more prominent place in your thinking by memorizing it, meditating on it, studying it, believing it, and obeying it, thereby drawing closer to the God who loves you and allowing Him to release His power in your life as you serve and follow Him.

A Prayer of Adoration

Oh, the depth of the riches both of Your wisdom and knowledge, O God! How unsearchable are Your judgments and Your ways are past finding out. Your greatness cannot be imagined. You are greater than all language, and no words can express your majesty. You are above all, outside of all, and beyond all I can even imagine. You are without limits. When I speak of You I cannot refer to amount or size or weight, for You are beyond measure. You are not less or more, large or small. You are simply God, the infinite One. A human mind has no capacity to comprehend You. What I can do is praise, adore, and worship You.

—Robert Savage

$\mathscr{S}$TILL CHANGING AND GROWING...

⟡

Grow in the grace and knowledge
of our Lord and Savior Jesus
Christ. To Him be the glory both
now and forever. Amen.

2 PETER 3:18

$\mathscr{D}$O YOU EVER STOP TO THINK ABOUT what was happening in your life ten years ago? What was happening then to cause you to grow as a Christian and in your trust in God? What follows is how God used one of those unexplainable, un-understandable events to ensure that I still loved Him and leaned on Him!

⟡

"I SURVIVED THE 6.8 NORTHRIDGE EARTHQUAKE!" That's what the Los Angeles sweatshirts heralded. But I don't need that kind of reminder. January 17, 1994, is a morning I will never forget....

Knowing that the week would be busy, I set the alarm to get up early—four in the morning. But this particular day I indulged in 20 extra minutes of rest. I was tempted to sleep in even more because Jim was gone, but I got up and made my way downstairs. I dropped my robe and slippers on a dining room chair and went into the kitchen to fill my teapot and boil water.

The first thing I saw in the kitchen was a stack of newspapers sitting on the counter, ready for the weekly trash pickup later that morning. For some reason, I decided to put them into our recycling bin before I filled the teakettle and got the water boiling. Gathering the papers, I walked toward the entryway door. As I reached for the doorknob, I was suddenly thrown against the wall. I looked up at the entryway light above me, which was swinging wildly... before it suddenly went dark. The electricity was out within a split second of the ground's first jolt.

"It's an earthquake!" Plaster fell on my head, and I was overwhelmed by the terrifying roar and rumble of the earth, sounds of splitting boards, collapsing block walls, shattering glass, falling furniture, and the slam of a tidal wave from the backyard pool against the sliding glass door. "This is the BIG one! I have to get out of this house!" Groping in the dark, I finally felt the doorknob in my hand. Now all I had to do was find and unlock the dead bolt. But finding it made no difference. The quake was twisting and contorting the door. I cried, "God, I can't get out!"

Between the thrusts and rolls of the earth, I managed to open the door. I dropped the newspapers and ran barefoot and in my nightshirt out of the house. At the end of our driveway, I fought to remain standing for the remaining eight horrific seconds of the magnitude 6.8 quake. Neighbors flooded out of their homes, and we stood in clusters, literally holding each other up as the giant aftershocks began rumbling through, attacking our homes as well as our nerves.

For two-and-a-half hours in the early-morning darkness, we huddled under blankets and waited in our cars. Behind us, the black sky burned with a sick orange hue. We found out later that 40 mobile homes two miles across the freeway had burned to the ground. Then we heard—and felt—a new sound. Three booming explosions shook our cars as the gas main on our street ignited. Now the sky in front of us burned with the same awful glow we had seen in the distance.

At last, the sun began to rise. I was shaking from the cold, the unending aftershocks, and the adrenaline racing through my body. I was also dreading going back into our home. I couldn't imagine what the inside must be like. It was then that a verse of Scripture came to mind—"This is the day which the Lord hath made; we will rejoice and be glad in it." But how could I rejoice, Lord? How could I be glad for this?

Two hours and 29 minutes after the initial quake, Jim drove into the driveway, returning from his Army Reserve weekend. We entered the house. It was then that God used each of the six scriptures in this book in new ways in my life.

Making a pathway to the kitchen, we saw that part of the ceiling had fallen in and that all of our cupboards were open. The dishwasher and drawers had also flown open. Broken dishes were in the sink and on the floor, the counters, and the stove. I exclaimed, "Jim, what if I had been in the kitchen? I would have been buried, injured, and cut to slivers! What if I had lighted the burner to boil water for my tea? There could have been a fire, an explosion, and our house could have burned to the ground! What if...?"

And Jim—faithful friend, wonderful husband, godly leader, and reader of the manuscript for this book—said, "Liz, it's time to practice what you preach. Remember Philippians 4:8? 'Whatsoever things are true [or real]...think on these things.' Liz, what is true? What is real? You weren't in the kitchen." This reminder was repeated throughout the next several days as we worked our way through our home.

Finally we forced the door to my office open, and when we did so, we saw that it was the site of the greatest destruction. My office! My sanctuary! When my daughter Katherine saw it, she burst into tears, knowing that I sometimes spent up to 18 hours a day in that room. Then it was her turn. She imagined, "Mom, what if...?" I had already beaten her to that thought. "What if I had been in that room? If I had gotten up at four, I would have been sitting on the couch there with my Bible, prayer book, and tea. And I would have been buried, probably killed by the seven-foot wall unit, loaded with books, bookends, and office equipment, that had shattered as it fell on my couch. What if...?"

Again God's Spirit used Philippians 4:8 to remind me to think on what is true or real and to draw closer to Him. I had not been in my office. I was safe. I was alive. God had protected me. That was true. That was real.

In the aftermath of the quake, I found that all I wanted to do was sit in numb fear, waiting for the next aftershock and watching hour after hour of horrifying but mesmerizing news coverage. But through Matthew 6:34, Christ called me to deal with today and not be anxious about tomorrow...

or the next aftershock. So I forced myself to make a list of things to do and to start doing them. I focused on the work at hand, not on the fears of the future.

Beyond these fears for my safety, I worried about the financial implications of the damage to our home, how rebuilding would interrupt daily living, and the setbacks that would result in my already too-busy schedule. My list of fears and worries went on and on. But again and again God offered me relief, peace, and hope through Matthew 6:34, where He called me not to worry.

God was also telling me through Philippians 3:13 and 14 to forget what lies behind and reach for what is ahead. The earthquake was over. I needed to address the tasks at hand and press on. I had to quit looking back.

I also had to resist the temptation to ask, "Why, God? What is going on? What are You doing?" God used Romans 8:28 to offer me daily reassurance that He causes all things to work together for good. Yes, the earthquake was destructive and horrible, and the aftermath continues to be horrible, but already I'm seeing God bring some good out of it. How?

We have grown closer to our neighbors as well as our family members. Katherine and Courtney, ages 23 and 24, thought first of us, as we did of them. We wanted to be together, see each other, spend time with one another, and pray together. Jim's mother's home suffered no damage, and she has taken us in, cooked for us, and provided a haven of peace and order. God is working good out of the bad. I am seeing beauty arise from ashes, experiencing joy despite sorrow, and finding reasons to praise despite the heaviness. And I'm sure that for years we will be discovering how God is working good from this rubble.

And so many of us are dealing with rubble right now. Just last night I encouraged other women with the promise of Jeremiah 29:11 and its meaning to me during the 11 days since the earthquake. God has used this passage to call me to focus on Him and His promise of future good. He has awakened in me, His child, fresh confidence for handling the far-from-ideal present.

And, finally, God is using the precious truth of Romans 11:33 to teach me new lessons about yielding to His wisdom, trusting Him in the dark (both literal and figurative!), submitting to His judgments, resting in His knowledge of all things, and accepting the mysterious, the unexplainable, the unacceptable. Because earthquakes are in God's domain, I am daily learning more about letting God be God.

Yes, I survived the 6.8 Northridge earthquake! And these last 11 days have been quite an experience. I have spent one night sleeping in the car, one night on the floor, and nine nights on the couch, fully clothed with my shoes on and the door open. For five days I had no makeup and wore the same clothes, and I went six days without a shower. For two days we had no electricity and for ten days no gas, no heat, and no water. For ten days, we carried pool water inside to flush the toilet, and I brushed my teeth outside using a pan of water.

But I have also spent those same 11 days placing my faith and trust in God over and over again—rather than in my shaky thoughts and emotions. During these 11 days, I have found myself loving God with all my mind in new and greater ways. I have also seen Him use the six powerful scriptures presented in this book to remind me of His great love for me. And now I extend to you a fresh invitation to discover the riches of God's love for you and of these wonderful promises that He can use to help you handle whatever comes your way. He has certainly used them in my life!

∾

That was ten years ago, and so much more has happened since then: the deaths of all of Jim's and my parents, the marriages of our two daughters, the arrival of six grandchildren, Jim's military activation to the war in Bosnia, several moves, the launching of a writing and speaking ministry by both Jim and me, not to mention being in Manhattan on September 11, 2001…and, last but not least, weathering Hurricane Jeanne this past weekend while speaking in Florida. With each of these events, I have continued to fall back upon the truths of God's Word and to claim again and again these same six promises from God in the trials and tribulations in my life.

I pray that this book and my earthquake story about the application of these six promises from God were helpful to you. As long as we are alive and walking with the Lord, God's Word assures us that God is in control and that, by His grace, we are still changing, growing ever closer to Him in our daily lives.

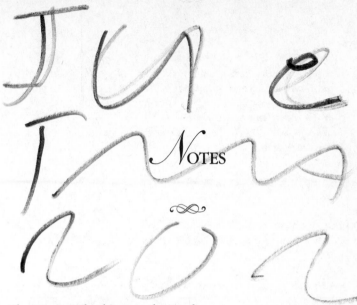

Notes

Chapter 1—Thinking on the Truth

1. Colorado Health Net, http://www.coloradohealthnet.org/depression/depression_facts.htm, 3/10/99.
2. Carole Mayhall, *From the Heart of a Woman* (Colorado Springs: Navpress, 1977), pp. 27-31; and Jim Downing, *Meditation: The Bible Tells You How* (Colorado Springs: NavPress, 1981).
3. Lorne Sanny, *Memorize the Word* (Chicago: The Moody Bible Institute of Chicago, 1980), 1-800-621-7105.

Chapter 2—Thinking the Truth About...God and His Word

1. Charles Caldwell Ryrie, *The Ryrie Study Bible* (Chicago: Moody Press, 1978), p. 30.

Chapter 3—Thinking the Truth About...Others

1. John C. Pollock, *A Foreign Devil in China: The Story of Dr. L. Nelson Bell, An American Surgeon in China* (Grand Rapids, MI: Zondervan Publishing House, 1971), p. 183.

Chapter 4—Thinking the Truth About...the Future

1. Charles F. Pfeiffer and Everett F. Harrison, eds., *The Wycliffe Bible Commentary* (Chicago: Moody Press, 1990), p. 1330.
2. Both quotes from Elisabeth Elliot, *Let Me Be a Woman* (Wheaton, IL: Tyndale House Publishers, Inc., 1977), p. 42.

Chapter 5—Thinking the Truth About...the Past and the Present

1. John MacArthur, *The MacArthur Study Bible* (Nashville: Word Bibles, 1996), p. 809.

Chapter 6—Taking Every Thought Captive

1. Charles F. Pfeiffer and Everett F. Harrison, eds., *The Wycliffe Bible Commentary* (Chicago: Moody Press, 1973), p. 1330.

Chapter 7—Focusing on Today

1. Gail MacDonald, *High Call, High Privilege* (Wheaton, IL: Tyndale House Publishers, Inc., 1982), pp. 30-34.
2. Ibid.
3. Ibid.
4. Ibid.

Chapter 8—Scaling the Mountain of Today

1. Ray and Anne Ortlund, *The Best Half of Life* (Waco, TX: Word, 1987), p. 24.
2. Ibid., p. 67.
3. Carole Mayhall, *Lord, Teach Me Wisdom* (Colorado Springs: Navpress, 1979), p. 155.
4. H.D.M. Spence and Joseph S. Exell, eds., *The Pulpit Commentary*, vol. 15 (Grand Rapids: Wm. B. Eerdmans Publishing Company, 1978), p. 239.
5. Albert M. Wells, Jr., *Inspiring Quotations, Contemporary & Classical* (Nashville: Thomas Nelson Publishers, 1988), p. 209.

Chapter 10—Living Out of God's Grace

1. Elisabeth Elliot, *Twelve Baskets of Crumbs* (Nashville: Pilar Books for Abingdon, 1976), p. 18.
2. Elisabeth Elliot, *Through Gates of Splendor* (New York: Harper & Brothers Publishers, 1957), p. 196.
3. Ibid.
4. Elliot, *Twelve Baskets of Crumbs*, p. 18.
5. Ibid., pp. 21-22.
6. Ibid., p. 20.
7. Edith Schaeffer, *The Tapestry* (Waco, TX: Word Books, 1981), pp. 613-638.
8. Ibid.
9. Ibid.
10. Ibid.
11. Ibid.
12. Ibid.
13. Schaeffer, *The Tapestry*, pp. 613-638.
14. Ibid.
15. Ibid.
16. Ibid.

Chapter 11—Remembering to Forget

1. Robert Jamieson, A.R. Fausset, David Brown, *Commentary on the Whole Bible* (Grand Rapids, MI: Zondervan Publishing House, 1973), p. 1310.
2. Kenneth S. Wuest, *Wuest's Word Studies from the Greek New Testament,* vol. 2 (Grand Rapids, MI: Wm. B. Eerdmans Publishing Company, 1973), pp. 97-98.
3. William Hendriksen, *New Testament Commentary — Exposition of Philippians* (Grand Rapids, MI: Baker Book House, 1975), p. 173.
4. Wuest, *Wuest's Word Studies,* vol. 2, pp. 97-98.
5. F.B. Meyer, *Devotional Commentary on Philippians* (Grand Rapids, MI: Kregel Publications, 1979), pp. 183-84.
6. E.M. Blaiklock, *The Acts of the Apostles, An Historical Commentary* (Grand Rapids, MI: Wm. B. Eerdmans Publishing Company, 1976), p. 79.
7. William Barclay, *The Acts of the Apostles,* rev. ed. (Philadelphia: The Westminster Press, 1976), p. 64.
8. Corrie ten Boom, *Tramp for the Lord* (Fort Washington, PA: Christian Literature Crusade and Old Tappan, NJ: Fleming H. Revell Company, 1974), p. 55.

Chapter 12—Finding the Gold

1. Norman Grubb, *C.T. Studd* (Grand Rapids, MI: Zondervan Publishing House, 1946), pp. 50-69.
2. Charles R. Swindoll, *Growing Strong Through the Seasons of Life* (Portland, OR: Multnomah Press, 1983), pp. 315-16.
3. H.D.M. Spence and Joseph S. Exell, eds., *The Pulpit Commentary,* vol. 20 (Grand Rapids, MI: Wm. B. Eerdmans Publishing Company, 1978), pp. 131, 138.
4. William Barclay, *The Letters to the Philippians, Colossians, and Thessalonians,* rev. ed. (Philadelphia: The Westminster Press, 1975), p. 66.
5. Helen Roseveare, *He Gave Us a Valley* (Downers Grove, IL: InterVarsity Press, 1976).
6. Elisabeth Elliot, *Through Gates of Splendor* (New York: Harper & Brothers Publishers, 1957).
7. Corrie ten Boom, *Tramp for the Lord* (Fort Washington, PA: Christian Literature Crusade and Old Tappan, NJ: Fleming H. Revell Company, 1974).

Chapter 13—Going On and On and On

1. William Barclay, *The Letters to the Philippians, Colossians, and Thessalonians,* rev. ed. (Philadelphia: The Westminster Press, 1975), p. 66.

Chapter 15—Keep on Keeping On

1. H.D.M. Spence and Joseph S. Exell, eds., *The Pulpit Commentary*, vol. 20 (Grand Rapids, MI: Wm. B. Eerdmans Publishing Company, 1978), p. 152.

2. Ralph P. Martin, *Tyndale New Testament Commentaries, The Epistle of Paul to the Philippians* (Grand Rapids, MI: Wm. B. Eerdmans Publishing Company, 1976), pp. 152-54.

3. As cited in Carole Mayhall, *Lord of My Rocking Boat* (Colorado Springs: NavPress, 1983), pp. 41-42.

4. As cited in Ray and Anne Ortlund, *The Best Half of Life* (Waco, TX: Word Books, 1987), p. 44.

5. Spence and Exell, eds., *Pulpit Commentary*, vol. 20, pp. 151-52.

Chapter 16—Pressing Toward God's Purpose

1. Pamela Rosewell, *The Five Silent Years of Corrie ten Boom* (Grand Rapids, MI: Zondervan Publishing House, 1986).

2. Shirley Price, *God's Plan for the Wife and Mother* (22422 Kathryn Ave., Torrance, CA 90505, 1976).

3. Cathy Guisewite, *Cathy* comic strip, *L.A. Times*, 1992.

Chapter 17—Trusting the Lord

1. Don Baker, *Pain's Hidden Purpose* (Portland, OR: Multnomah Press, 1983), p. 69.

2. H.D.M. Spence and Joseph S. Exell, eds., *The Pulpit Commentary*, vol. 18 (Grand Rapids, MI: Wm. B. Eerdmans Publishing Company, 1977), p. 212.

3. Robert Jamieson, A.R. Fausset, and David Brown, *Commentary on the Whole Bible* (Grand Rapids, MI: Zondervan Publishing House, 1973), p. 1163.

Chapter 18—Knowing God's Promise

1. John F. MacArthur, *The MacArthur New Testament Commentary, Romans 1-8* (Chicago: Moody Press, 1991), p. 473.

2. Ibid.

3. Dwight L. Moody, *Notes from My Bible and Thoughts from My Library* (Grand Rapids, MI: Baker Book House, 1979), p. 256.

4. Kenneth S. Wuest, *Wuest's Word Studies from the Greek New Testament*, vol. 1 (Grand Rapids, MI: Wm. B. Eerdmans Publishing Company, 1974), p. 143, emphasis added.

Chapter 19—Becoming Faith Oriented

1. Ney Bailey, *Faith Is Not a Feeling* (San Bernardino, CA: Here's Life Publishers, Inc., 1978), pp. 1-5.

2. Charles R. Swindoll, *Joseph: From Pit to Pinnacle,* Bible Study Guide (Fullerton, CA: Insight for Living, 1982), p. i.
3. *Life Application Bible — The Living Bible* (Wheaton, IL: Tyndale House Publishers, Inc., and Youth for Christ/USA, 1988), p. 1587.

Chapter 20—Navigating the Maze of Life
1. Alan Redpath, *Victorious Christian Living* (Old Tappan, NJ: Fleming H. Revell, 1951), p. 166.
2. M.R. DeHaan and Henry G. Bosch, *Bread for Each Day* (Grand Rapids, MI: Zondervan Publishing House, 1962), June 23.

Chapter 21—Enduring Difficult Times
1. Irving L. Jensen, *Everyman's Bible Commentary, Jeremiah* (Chicago: Moody Press, 1966), p. 83.
2. Mrs. Charles E. Cowman, *Streams in the Desert,* vol. 2 (Grand Rapids, MI: Zondervan Publishing House, 1966), p. 368.

Chapter 22—Bearing Fruit During Difficult Times
1. John W. Cowart, *People Whose Faith Got Them into Trouble* (Downers Grove, IL: InterVarsity Press, 1990), pp. 76-77.
2. Ibid., pp. 73, 76.
3. Norman Grubb, *C.T. Studd* (Grand Rapids, MI: Zondervan Publishing House, 1946), p. 161.
4. Cowart, *People Whose Faith Got Them into Trouble,* p. 112.
5. Ibid., pp. 111-12.
6. Ibid., p. 113.
7. *Life Application Bible* (Wheaton, IL: Tyndale House Publishers, 1988), p. 1089.
8. Curtis Vaughan, *The Old Testament Books of Poetry from 26 Translations* (Grand Rapids, MI: Zondervan Bible Publishers, 1973), p. 220.
9. The Septuagint, the Greek translation of the Old Testament.
10. E.M. Blaiklock, *Psalms for Living,* vol. 1 (Philadelphia and New York: A.J. Holman, a division of J.B. Lippincott Co., 1977), p. 94.

Chapter 23 — Becoming God's Masterpiece
1. Edith Schaeffer, *What Is a Family?* (Old Tappan, NJ: Fleming H. Revell Company, 1975), pp. 183-84.

Chapter 24—Living Out God's Promise
1. H.D.M. Spence and Joseph S. Exell, eds., *The Pulpit Commentary,* vol. 11 (Grand Rapids, MI: Wm. B. Eerdmans Publishing Company, 1978), p. 587.

Chapter 25—Responding to Life's Turning Points

1. C.C. Carlson, *Corrie ten Boom: Her Life, Her Faith* (Old Tappan, NJ: F.H. Revell Co., 1983), p. 83.
2. Harold D. Foos, *James: Faith in Practice* (Chicago: Moody Correspondence School, 1984), p. 29.
3. James M. Freeman, *Manners and Customs of the Bible* (Plainfield, NJ: Logos International, 1972), p. 231.
4. Charles Caldwell Ryrie, *The Ryrie Study Bible* (Chicago: Moody Press, 1978), p. 1544.
5. Gien Karssen, *Her Name Is Woman* (Colorado Springs: NavPress, 1975), p. 131.
6. Curtis Vaughan, *The New Testament from 26 Translations* (Grand Rapids, MI: Zondervan Publishing House, 1967), p. 215.

Chapter 26—Majoring on the Minors

1. A.W. Tozer, *The Knowledge of the Holy* (New York: Harper & Row Publishers, 1961), p. 10.

Chapter 27—Trusting God in the Dark

1. A.W. Tozer, *The Knowledge of the Holy* (New York: Harper & Row Publishers, 1961), p. 66.
2. Ibid., p. 68.
3. Oswald Chambers, *He Shall Glorify Me* (Fort Washington, PA: Christian Literature Crusade, 1946), p. 52.
4. Robert Jamieson, A.R. Fausset, and David Brown, *Commentary on the Whole Bible* (Grand Rapids, MI: Zondervan Publishing Company, 1977), p. 1173.
5. Charles F. Pfeiffer and Everett F. Harrison, eds., *The Wycliffe Bible Commentary* (Chicago: Moody Press, 1973), p. 1219.

$\mathcal{I}$f you've benefited from *Loving God with All Your Mind,*
you'll want the companion volume

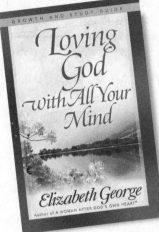

$\mathcal{L}$oving $\mathcal{G}$od
with
$\mathcal{A}$ll $\mathcal{Y}$our $\mathcal{M}$ind

Growth
and
Study Guide

This guide offers additional scriptures, thought-provoking questions, reflective studies, and personal and practical applications that will improve your thought life.

This growth and study guide is perfect for both
personal and group use.

Loving God with All Your Mind Growth and Study Guide
is available at your local Christian bookstore
or can be ordered from:

Jim and Elizabeth George Ministries
P.O. Box 2879
Belfair, WA 98528
1-800-542-4611
www.elizabethgeorge.com

About the Author

Elizabeth George is a bestselling author who has more than 4.8 million books in print. She is a popular speaker at Christian women's events. Her passion is to teach the Bible in a way that changes women's lives. For information about Elizabeth's speaking ministry, to sign up for her mailings, or to purchase her books visit her website:

Jim and Elizabeth George Ministries
P.O. Box 2879
Belfair, WA 98528

1-800-542-4611

www.ElizabethGeorge.com

BIBLE STUDIES *for* BUSY WOMEN

Character Studies

Old Testament Studies

New Testament Studies

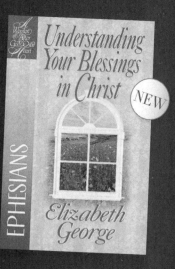

A Woman's High Calling

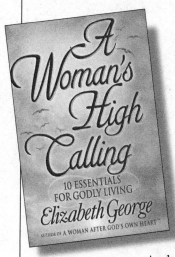

Is the cry of your heart to exchange the clutter and chaos of everyday life for a simple focus on what's really important? If so, there's no better place to look for help than the Bible. There we find the essentials God values most in a woman. *A Woman's High Calling* explores the 10 essentials for godly living as presented in Titus 2:3-5, including wisdom, purity, ministry, godly behavior, and love of home.

Start simplifying your life right now by putting these priorities into practice in all that you do...and experience the joy that comes from living in a way that pleases God and fulfills His purposes for your life.

❦

Books by Elizabeth George

- Beautiful in God's Eyes
- Finding God's Path Through Your Trials
- Following God with All Your Heart
- Life Management for Busy Women
- Loving God with All Your Mind
- A Mom After God's Own Heart
- Quiet Confidence for a Woman's Heart
- The Remarkable Women of the Bible
- Small Changes for a Better Life
- Walking with the Women of the Bible
- A Wife After God's Own Heart
- Windows into the Word of God
- A Woman After God's Own Heart®
- A Woman After God's Own Heart®
  Deluxe Edition
- A Woman After God's Own Heart®—A
  Daily Devotional
- A Woman After God's Own Heart®
  Collection
- A Woman's Call to Prayer
- A Woman's High Calling
- A Woman's Walk with God
- A Young Woman After God's
  Own Heart
- A Young Woman After God's
  Own Heart—A Devotional
- A Young Woman's Call to Prayer
- A Young Woman's Guide to Making
  Right Choices
- A Young Woman's Walk with God

Study Guides

- Beautiful in God's Eyes
  Growth & Study Guide
- Finding God's Path Through Your Trials
  Growth & Study Guide
- Following God with All Your Heart
  Growth & Study Guide
- Life Management for Busy Women
  Growth & Study Guide
- Loving God with All Your Mind
  Growth & Study Guide
- A Mom After God's Own Heart
  Growth & Study Guide
- The Remarkable Women of the Bible
  Growth & Study Guide
- Small Changes for a Better Life
  Growth & Study Guide
- A Wife After God's Own Heart
  Growth & Study Guide
- A Woman After God's Own Heart®
  Growth & Study Guide
- A Woman's Call to Prayer
  Growth & Study Guide
- A Woman's High Calling
  Growth & Study Guide
- A Woman's Walk with God
  Growth & Study Guide

Children's Books

- God's Wisdom for Little Girls
- A Little Girl After God's Own Heart

Books by Jim & Elizabeth George

- God Loves His Precious Children
- God's Wisdom for Little Boys
- A Little Boy After God's Own Heart

Books by Jim George

- The Bare Bones Bible® Handbook
- The Bare Bones Bible® Handbook
  for Teens
- The Bare Bones Bible® Bios
- A Husband After God's Own Heart
- A Man After God's Own Heart
- The Remarkable Prayers of the Bible
- A Young Man After God's Own Heart